HE Knows My Name
A DAILY DEVOTIONAL

by Sandy Wakefield

Copyright © 2017 Sandy Wakefield

All Rights Reserved

**Dedicated to my God, and my Rock,
Jesus Christ
and to Him be the glory.**

He is the author and finisher of my faith.

TABLE OF CONTENTS

JANUARY

January 1

Jeremiah 6:17

I set a watchmen over you, saying, Hearken to the sound of the trumpet. KJV

When I created you, I created you in order, not chaos. When you are feeling or sensing that chaotic stress in the mind or spirit, stop and take a moment to withdraw with Me. I will still your soul. This is

HE KNOWS MY NAME

where your strength comes from, your relationship with Me. Tap into My strength and I will rock your world. Trust Me and I can carry you through anything. All things are possible to him that believes, only because I am able.

January 2

Jeremiah 6:16

Stand ye in the ways, and see, and ask for the old paths, where is the good way, and walk therein, and ye shall find rest for your souls. KJV

The church world is always looking for new ways to reach souls. The bargain basement, the sundae showers, the food and events unlimited - always seem to be great ideas. You may gather a crowd. You may reach some or trick some into returning for a short while. However, the fruit that remains are the ones you will reach with one on one witnessing. Some will be strangers. Some will be coworkers. Some will be family members. All will have deeper rooted conversions because of your taking the time with them to share Christ. It's a different dynamic. Keep your head up and pay attention to whom I would have you speak to today. I need your hands and feet to carry the gospel to the hurting. I will give you the words to speak and the opportunity will present itself.

January 3

Wait

Lamentations 3:25

The Lord is good unto them that wait for him, to the soul that seeketh him. KJV

I understand your frustration. Can't you see though, 'waiting' for Me is not quite what you are doing when you are throwing a fit for Me to move in your timing. I see the situation. I hear your cry. Waiting on Me is trusting My timing as well, without telling Me off while you 'wait'. So, in the desperate times, seek Me. Get to know Me. Learn of Me. Speak to Me. Ask. Listen to Me. It's ok to speak of Me. In fact, I'll bless that and bring you fruit right in the midst of the explosions of chaos in your life.

Lamentations 3:26

It is good that a man should both hope and quietly wait for the salvation of the Lord.   KJV

January 4

Hope

Lamentations 3:22-24

It is of the Lord's mercies that we are not consumed, because his compassions fail not. They are new every morning; great is thy faithfulness. The Lord is my portion, saith my soul; therefore will I hope in him.   KJV

Hope truly is an amazing thing. Faith is the evidence of still having hope, before the hope is realized. When you give up hope, well what have you got? So as with faith. Without faith there is no relationship with Me. Because only with faith can you enter the kingdom of God. My compassions never ever fail. They are new every single morning. I will never give up on you. I seek for you daily. Take time for your relationship with Me. I will pour My mercies out upon you when you come to Me with that hope. Leave the jadedness of life at the foot of the cross. Look up, and have faith in Me. You are Mine.

January 5

The Lord My Banner

Lamentations 3:40-41

Let us search and try our ways, and turn again to the Lord. Let us lift up our heart with our hands unto God in the heavens.   KJV

Just a question. When was the last time you lifted up your heart and raised your hands towards Me in heaven during your closet prayer? I know you do in church. What about when it's just you and Me and there is no one else to see. This is a surrendered spirit. This one who worships in the open and worships in private, this is the one I can bless. Take time in worship. It will flood your soul with My Holy Spirit. The access to heaven that it will bring will boggle your mind.

Exodus 17:11-15

And it came to pass, when Moses held up his hand, that Israel prevailed; and when he let down his hand, Amalek prevailed. But Moses' hands were heavy; and they took a stone, and put it under him, and sat there on; and Aaron and Hur stayed up his hands, the one on the one side, and the other on the other side; and his hands were steady until the going down of the sun. And Joshua discomfited Amalek and his people with the edge of the sword. And the Lord said to Moses, write this for a memorial in a book, and rehearse it in the ears of Joshua: for I will utterly put out the remembrance of Amalek from under heaven. And Moses built an altar, and called the name of it Jehovahnissi: That is, the LORD my banner.   KJV

January 6

Isaiah 30:15

...in returning and rest shall ye be saved; in quietness and in confidence shall be your strength..   KJV

You long for rest, you say, time and again. Quit running around doing what you think should be done. Take time for Me. I will bring you strength. Come to prayer, rest in salvation, do today what I have called you to. My burden really and truly is lighter. Be still, be quiet, have confidence in My calling for your life, this is where you will abundantly grow and prosper beyond measure. Trust Me again. The world has tons of distractions. You have many responsibilities. I can help you meet the needs of your responsibilities and use you to reach a lost and dying world as well.

January 7

1 Peter 5:6

Humble yourselves therefore under the mighty hand of God, that He may exalt you in due time.   KJV

Humbleness is a difficult trait for the human spirit. I've created you for so many things, and your strengths are abundant, I did that on purpose. You were created to have dominance over the earth.

However, you have ended up with zero dominance over sin and destruction. As sin entered in, your dominance over many things has eroded. This was the need for Christ. As He enters your physical body, with spiritual power, you become dominate again. Do not deceive yourselves when things seem to be going well. Always remember this is Christ - manifesting My power and strength in you, as you ask. You have no victories without Me. You win zero wars without Me. That is by design. Sin will satisfy for a season, but the end there of is always always destruction. Humility admits Christ is in control and all strength and power comes from Me. Humility allows Me to guide and direct your life. Show up in prayer this morning. Do not be so haughty to believe you can take care of the kingdom today in purity and strength without a touch of your Master's hand.

January 8

2 Corinthians 7:1

Having therefore these promises, dearly beloved, let us cleanse ourselves from all filthiness of the flesh and spirit, perfecting holiness in the fear of God.   KJV

Does it bother you when I ask you to be like Me? Perfecting holiness. Think on those words. Would you honor Me today? Would you honor Me by doing the things I ask of you? For example, perfecting holiness? If you ask Me, I will help you with that. Live undefiled, set yourself apart from gossip, pornography, violence, alcohol, drugs, wickedness, mean spirits, and hard-hearted people. Make yourself available to speak My Word into the wounded souls, the afflicted, the poor, the empty, the depressed, the one that is down and out. Then rest at the end of your day and ponder the difference in your own spirit when you do these things. This, my dear, is growth and maturity. I am entrusting this ministry of your generation, in your corner of the earth, to you.

January 9

Jeremiah 39:17-18

But I will deliver thee in that day, saith the Lord; and thou shalt not be given into the hand of the men of whom thou art afraid. For I will surely deliver thee, and thou shalt not fall by the sword, but thy life shall be for a prey unto thee; because thou hast put thy trust in me, saith the Lord. KJV

Fear paralyzes. It is a spirit. You must rise above it. I will deliver you, you do not ever have to doubt that. I've made you that promise time and again, personally, through My Word. I am not a man that I would lie to you. When I speak it, it will come to pass. Never doubt that. I am here. In crisis of faith, turn to My Word. Ask Me. I will show you the way. I long to be your compass of life. Follow Me. It's a wild ride, and you'll love it. Only those that risk and trust will find it the most thrilling.

January 10

Reconciliation

2 Corinthians 5:17-18

Therefore if any man be in Christ, he is a new creature; old things are passed away; behold, all things are become new. And all things are of God, who hath reconciled us to himself by Jesus Christ, and hath given to us the ministry of reconciliation. KJV

Reconciliation is a product of salvation. Without salvation, repentance through Christ, there is no reconciliation with Me. With no change in your life, the new creature birth, there is a lack of evidence of reconciliation with Me. How awful would it be to live out this human experience on earth and the end result being an enemy of Mine. For if you are neglectful of reconciliation with Christ, let Me make it clear you are My enemy. Be thankful for the cross. Thank Jesus, out loud, for the cross. For without it your attempts at reconciliation are useless. With it, you have salvation, rebirth, reconciliation, and eternal life. With it, you are given the power of a spoken word, inspired through My Holy Spirit, from My very nature that dwells within you, to reach others and offer them this astounding gift as well. Dwell on that for a while. Think on these things.

January 11

Jeremiah 39:18

"... You'll walk out of there safe and sound because you trusted me." GOD'S DECREE.

The Message

Trust is an amazing word. Your child trusts - that when you hold his hand and cross the road, he will make it safely to the other side. Your child trusts - that when he jumps you will catch him. Your child trusts - that when dinner time comes his belly will be full. Your child trusts - that when he asks for a drink of water, that you won't give him poison to drink. Your child trusts - that you love him.

In the world, as well meaning as parents are, good parents in many ways, often fail their children's trust. But I, I do not fail. I will catch you. I will feed you. I will quench your thirst with living waters. I will never lead you astray. You can trust these things so much that sometimes you forget what it was like without this trust in Me. Then when the pressure comes from a circumstance, all of a sudden you don't think you know My voice. Stay in prayer. Stay in My Word. I have much to teach you. But the most important today is trust. Trust My love for you. Listen, I am right here speaking. Take a moment, and listen.

January 12

Share - Even in the midst of trials

1 Thessalonians 5:18

In everything give thanks, for this is the will of God in Christ Jesus concerning you. KJV

If you are giving thanks even in the midst of trials it is easier to share the joy of Christ just in your attitude and spirit as you tell someone who Christ really is. If you take the time to speak My Word into someone else, even as you say, thank you God for this trial, help me to share your Word, then the joy that will flood your soul will many times be the very thing that turns the trial into a blessing. Watch and see what I will do when you are faithful to your calling even in the midst of the storms of life. My love is sufficient.

January 13

Luke 1:50-51

His mercy flows in wave after wave on those who are in awe before Him. He bared His arm and showed His strength, scattered the bluffing braggarts.   The Message

And His mercy is on them that fear Him from generation to generation. He hath shewed strength with his arm; he hath scattered the proud in the imagination of their hearts.   KJV

I want to unload My strength on you. It's tied to My mercy. Which is tied to your 'fear' of me as the translator spoke in the King James Version, or 'awe' of Me which the translator spoke in more recent times in The Message Version. Both are correct. I do not show mercy to those who refuse Me. I do not share My strength to those who care not to receive it on My terms. My strength is yours because you are Mine. Stay close to Me.

Romans 5:6

For when we were without strength, in due time Christ died for the ungodly. KJV

Christ arrives right on time to make this happen he didn't, and doesn't, wait for us to get ready. The Message

January 14

Philippians 4:13

I can do all things through Christ which strengtheneth me. KJV

Only through Christ's death and resurrection will you find the power to change. Paul came to this conclusion. You must as well. You will not find conversions without the power of Christ. You may find religious feel good people that say they have changed. But their hearts tell a different story. You will not find conversions without the power of Christ. That's why He died and rose again. To give you that power to change. Repent and follow Me. There is no other name in heaven given to men whereby they can be saved. Don't go for the okey doke. That's hell's lie. Always always share My name. Share My Word. Share My power. Or they will not be saved.

Revelation 21:4

And God shall wipe away all tears from their eyes; and there shall be no more death, neither sorrow, nor crying, neither shall there be any more pain: for the former things are passed away.   KJV

I prepare a home for you. I promised you this. I do not make junk. The floors will not fall in. You will not have to inspect the roof. No need for pest control. Your eyes have not seen, nor can you fathom, what awaits you in heaven. This means, your rewards are unfathomable. Stay faithful, stay pliable, trust and obey, one day at a time. All of heaven is cheering you on as you run your course. Finish with Me. No one enters but by Me. When I spoke, streets of gold, I meant it. And much more than that awaits you. If the streets, where you keep mere asphalt and dirt and mire, are made of gold, consider what the home and furnishings must be made of. Look up, your redemption draws nigh.

One day you'll be standing in your Father's house. And it will be the home of your dreams.

Anne Graham Lotz

Proverbs 15:31

Listen to good advice if you want to live well, an honored guest among wise men and women. The Message

The ear that heareth the reproof of life abideth among the wise. KJV

Abiding among the wise, an honored guest among My wise people. Think on this. I want you 'living' with reproof, waking up to and going to bed and sleeping with, and fellowshipping with during your waking hours, good advice. That means always learning. I want you studying and learning all the time. It never ends. It is all the time. Seek, find, treasure, ponder, and then look for more. This is how you will grow. People who think they know everything and are not open to learn are stunted in growth. It's like prying and planting a seed in a rock. Ah, but the fertile soil, the rich earth of a life willing to be corrected, is where My fruit shall abound.

January 17

The End is Near

Galatians 6:9

"And let us not be weary in well doing: for in due season we shall reap, if we faint not." **KJV**

Yes, those who finish, those who endure, those who keep their eyes on Me, those are the ones fit for the Kingdom. How many have you and I watched fall to the wayside. Many because of lack of growth, many because all their energies are given on the wrong tasks, tasks that I have not called them to. Growth and endurance and strength come from obedience to My calling. When you spend all you have, time, energy, resources, on your will, it will not only wear you down and make you unfit, it will cause you weakness. You will need all the growth and strength I am working in you, for your final race. Know you not that the end of the race is more energy spent than the beginning or the pace of one in the middle of his race trying to find his stride of persistency. When you are pushing that final push, the push you will need all your energies for, the time when many drop to the wayside, the weariness will prevail if you are unfit. Take time, fight distractions, pray and seek and obey Me, and be fit for the kingdom.

January 18

Psalms 123:1-2

Unto thee lift I up mine eyes, O thou that dwellest in the heavens. Behold, as the eyes of servants look unto the hand of their masters, and as the eyes of a maiden unto the hand of her mistress; so our eyes wait upon the Lord our God, until that he have mercy upon us.   KJV

As you wait for My Word today, spend time in prayer in the morning with Me. Start your day, begin your plans, with Me and My will on the tip of your finger, tongue, mind and spirit. When you plan with Me, your days will be much more fruitful. I am with you. That is not merely a cliché. That is truth. Here I am. I am right here. Look about you. Do you see all I have done for you to get your attention? I created you for fellowship with Me. It's in you. That need for fellowship with Me. Remember that little Sunday school song? "Life without Jesus, is like a donut, cause there's a hole in the middle of your heart". I created you that way on purpose, so you wouldn't forget Me. Sit down. Let's talk awhile.

January 19

When the Lord Utters His Voice

Jeremiah 51:16

When he uttereth his voice, there is a multitude of waters in the heavens; and he causeth the vapours to ascend from the ends of the earth; he maketh lightnings with rain, and bringeth forth the wind out of his treasures.   KJV

Ever wonder why man attempts to do so many things I have set aside for Me and Me alone to control? As your scientists on earth long to know and predict the weather, to control the outcomes, so you try feebly to control My perfect will for your life. You see so many different ways 'I' could fix 'your' circumstances. Take time for morning prayer, take time for fasting and seeking Me, then I can 'fix' your life. You've removed yourself so far from My will with yourself stuck on the throne, that you bind My hands until you repent and come close again. I am God. You are not. I see so many circumstances that your actions affect. You do not, you only see self. Pick up your head, lift your eyes, look at Me. Remember who I am. Repent, draw close again. I can fix this. I really am able. Come here, repent, then listen.

January 20

Jeremiah 20:11

But the Lord is with me as a mighty terrible one; therefore my persecutors shall stumble, and they shall not prevail; they shall be greatly ashamed; for they shall not prosper; their everlasting confusion shall never be forgotten. KJV

Many employed these days by corporations or companies that only look at the bottom line find themselves caught up in a culture of wrong and sin. Many times, this culture is so filthy the Christian cannot stay there. I will use many things to move you, however, sometimes I would like you to reach some of those involved before I move you. Witness, share the gospel, out loud and unashamed, I will bless you soon, but for right now, I need to use you in the midst of their vileness. This, like Jeremiah, will lead to persecutions. Trust Me. I will never let you down. Your deliverance is coming. Speak loud and speak clear. "God is not pleased with unrighteousness. You must maintain dignity and integrity if you wish your company and finances to prosper. Cheating, lying and stealing may work for a minute, but the foundation will definitely crumble. Take time to build something that will last."

January 21

Protector

Ps 71:1-5, 17

In thee, O Lord do I put my trust: let me never be put to confusion. Deliver me in thy righteousness, and cause me to escape: incline thine ear unto me. Be thou my strong habitation, whereunto I may continually resort: thou hast given commandment to save me; for thou art my rock and my fortress. Deliver me, O my God, out of the hand of the wicked, out of the hand of the unrighteousness and cruel man. For thou art my hope, O Lord God: thou art my trust from my youth. KJV

If I give you an armor, then you can be sure there is a need to be protected. David understood the need for protection. As he called upon Me in his youth, likewise in the seemingly unsurmountable battles as King, he learned the importance of My hand over his life. As I protected David, would I not also cover and protect you as well? Wear My armor. Clothe yourself in Me. The helmet of salvation, the breast plate of righteousness, shod those feet of yours with the gospel as it has been prepared for you. But remember always the full armor. The shield of faith in Me, gird and dress your loins in truth and trust Me in all circumstances to know I will protect and keep you.

January 22

Jeremiah 18:6

O house of Israel, cannot I do with you as this potter? saith the Lord, Behold, as the clay is in the potter's hand, so are ye in mine hand, ... KJV

For I would say unto you this day, if you would just allow Me to mold and shape you, I could revolutionize your life. I would make you a soul winner beyond your wildest dreams. People would stop and listen as you begin to speak of Me. I would direct your paths specifically where folks who long to hear My voice are. They are waiting for such a one that would speak to them of Me. They cry in the night in the prayers. They cry in the mornings in heartache. They lift up their voices to Me amongst the ash and ruin of their lives. Will you be someone who will discipline their life to follow My paths?

January 23

Jeremiah 15:19-21

This is how God answered me: "Take back those words, and I'll take you back. Then you'll stand tall before me. Use words truly and well. Don't stoop to cheap whining. Then, but only then, you'll speak for me. Let your words change them. Don't change your words to suit them. I'll turn you into a steel wall, impregnable. They'll attack you but won't put a dent in you because I'm at your side, defending and delivering." God's decree. "I'll deliver you from the grip of the wicked. I'll get you out of the clutch of the ruthless." The Message

When you speak, take time to think about what to say. Don't just say everything that floats through your head. This is where I say "be slow to speak". Let Me give you the words. This is where you will see fruit that will remain. Every person on this earth needs to hear what I have to say to them. When you speak for Me, allow Me to fill your mouth. Guard your words. They are so much more powerful than you could possibly comprehend. But speak. Speak to them for Me. I need you to be My voice in their ear.

January 24

Jeremiah 17:24-27

And it shall come to pass, if ye diligently hearken unto me, saith the Lord, .. hallow the sabbath day, to do no work therein; ... they shall come .. bringing in ... offerings ... sacrifices of praise, unto the house of the Lord. KJV

The completion of that scripture is worth a study. They shall come from the north, the south, the east, and the west to worship with you, if you will 'diligently' listen and obey Me concerning the sabbath day. It is to be set aside for My work. This day is to take time and remember where I have brought you from. Church attendance is critical in your walk with Me. Do not forsake the gathering of the people. It is your responsibility to find a church, and become a part of the community in that respect, so you can grow and come close to Me. Where else would you pray? Where else would you bring others that you are leading to Me and My kingdom to nurture and help their growth? Where else would you pay your tithe and offerings? Where else would you bring your sacrifice of praise? How will you know unless you are told, unless there is a preacher behind a pulpit to preach and teach the Word into your very life? There are life flowing wells of My Spirit in the earth. You must find your place lest you become stagnant and die.

John 14:1-4

Let not your heart be troubled: yes believe in God, believe also in Me. In My Father's house are many mansions: if it were not so, I would have told you. I go to prepare a place for you. And if I go and prepare a place for you, I will come again, and receive you unto Myself; that where I am, there ye may be also. And whither I go ye know, and the way ye know. **KJV**

I speak these words to bring encouragement to your weary soul. To give you a vision. To show you there are rewards. The greatest reward of coming home with Me will be of your being home with Me. My presence will be there. And do not try to dissect My words on this. When I say I am going to prepare a place for you, that is exactly what I mean. And you will meet Me face to face. Not in a glass darkly. Face to face. Trust Me. Your mind cannot comprehend nor fathom the rewards for those that diligently seek Me. I will come back for you. Stay steadfast, stay faithful.

Proverbs 26:2

You have as little to fear from an undeserved curse as from the dart of a wren or the swoop of a swallow. **The Message**

As the bird by wandering, as the swallow by flying, so the curse causeless shall not come. **KJV**

The devil masks things. As you make wonderful strides in the supernatural, he'll throw up torments in your mind. Past failures, past condemnations that have been dealt with over and over again. Do you trust Me or are you going to allow hell to steal your joy and cause you to be distracted from what you need to be doing today? I am not a God of confusion. When you are confused, and unsure if it is the Holy Spirit's convictions or hell's condemnations, draw close to Christ. Happy are they whose mind is stayed on Me. It is a renewing of the mind where you will find strength and peace. When you asked I forgave, and when I forgive, I forgive and start you on a new day. Forgiveness is real. Regrets are regrets. But give them to Me. You are not equipped to handle them constantly. That's why He died.

January 27

Blind but not Dumb

Mark 10:46-52

Vs 50 and casting away his garment, rose, and came to Jesus

Vs 52 Jesus said, Go thy way; thy faith has made you whole.   KJV

Consider the blind man that received his sight by the touch of Jesus' hand. Bartimaeus had never even met Jesus, let alone spoke to Him before. Yet I moved. I gave him that healing. Why? Did you see that cloak he used for his begging that he threw away, before Jesus even laid hands on him, or spoke to him? Now that! Delights Me!! This man gave Me opportunity to move. Believing in things not seen, that my child is faith. Give Me that opportunity in your life today. Toss it away, and I can heal. Look around and see what you cling so tightly to for your substance and pittance and toss it by faith. See what I won't do for you.

January 28

Proverbs 28:1

The wicked flee when no man pursueth; but the righteous are bold as a lion.   KJV

Fear is a powerful spirit unleashed in the earth. It causes men to do many things. It travels with selfishness. It is always self-preservation that is motivated when fear strikes. When I say 'do not fear' it is because I am trying to help you. When you allow this spirit to operate in your life you open a door to hell, and all that comes with it. Self is an enthroning that you allow in place of Me. When you take self, self-preservation, off of the throne of your life, freedom to serve Me replaces it. When you clothe yourself in the righteousness of Me, through repentance of sin, repentance of fear and unbelief and love of self, you are free indeed. Why? Because I set you free. Put on the garment of praise. Put it on. Pull it up and around you. Watch what I do in your life. It will rock your world!

January 29

1 Corinthians 1:18-21

For the preaching of the cross is to them that perish foolishness; but unto us which are saved it is the power of God. For it is written, I will destroy the wisdom of the wise, and will bring to nothing the understanding of the prudent. Where is the wise? Where is the scribe? Where is the disputed of the world? hath not God made foolish the wisdom of this world? For after that in the wisdom of God the world by wisdom knew not God, it pleased God by the foolishness of preaching to save them that believe. KJV

You have been saved from the nonsense of this world. You live in a godless generation. But you always have a hope of the gospel. I am not disillusioned by what the world does, I expect it. Paul's preaching always ended in a riot or revival. He didn't mind upsetting people. Do you? You must get this: they will not understand 'unless' they hear the gospel. The simple gospel confronts. It will turn even your own family against you. It brings division. If you compromise with them, you become dead religion. There is no other way but the

Son. I am God. I made the rules. You try to live by them. Do not bend to their ways. Act like a Christian-- give praises to Me for the things I do, out loud, in front of them. Be foolish, it's their only hope. Let your life be a testimony. Let them see there is a difference. I chose you, not because you're brilliant, but because you're foolish, to show up the worldly wise. Go... make a difference in somebody's life today.

January 30

Stand Your Ground

Ephesians 6:13-14.

....having done all, to stand. Stand.... KJV

13-18. Be prepared. You're up against far more than you can handle on your own. Take all the help you can get, every weapon God has issued, so that when it's all over but the shouting you'll still be on your feet. Truth, righteousness, peace, faith and salvation are more than just words. Learn how to apply them. You'll need them throughout your life. God's word is an indispensable weapon. In the same way, prayer is essential in this ongoing warfare. Pray hard and long. Pray for your brothers and sisters. Keep your eyes open. Keep each other's spirits up so that no one falls behind or drops out.   The Message

When you allow yourself to get too worn or weak without prayer or My Word you are placing yourself in imminent danger. Never never ever give up. When I say, having done all --- just stand -- that doesn't mean stand and do nothing. It means 'do all'. Put the armor on. 'Do it.' Then stand. Because you will be standing in Me. Those who stand in Me will be victorious. Trust Me. Stand in Me. When you are weary. When you are sick. When you are tempted. When you feel hateful. When all of hell seems to be pulling and shooting at you. Attacks seem to be coming from everywhere. You are very likely right in the midst of My will. Hell will oppose. Stand. But put that armor on first. I will stand with you. Look for Me. I'm right here.

I won't lay a burden on you that is unmanageable. Head up, eyes forward, I am in control.

January 31

Proverbs 1:33.

First pay attention to Me, and then relax. Now you can take it easy --- you're in good hands.

The Message

But whoso harkeneth unto Me shall dwell safely, and shall be quiet from fear of evil. KJV

Folks who obey Me, and seek My training will experience the privilege of being in very good hands. How many times have I whispered in your ear, "trust Me". That's because I want you to trust Me. Ask Me. Then trust Me. You have My Word on it!!!! And by the way, that's the best relaxation you will ever know.

FEBRUARY

February 1

Psalms 61:1-3

Hear my cry, O God; attend unto my prayer. From the end of the earth will I cry unto thee, when my heart is overwhelmed; lead me to the rock that is higher than I. For thou hast been a shelter for me, and a strong tower from the enemy.   KJV

When you get the feeling I am not listening, or your prayers are hitting the ceiling and bouncing around. When you do not see answers to your prayers. Speak to Me with this scripture. It's ok to pray with scripture. It's ok to pick up your bible, walk the floor, and with great passion read My Word aloud. Speaking it to Me, I will bring it closer to your heart. The spoken word is a powerful weapon. Do not discount it. You speak things into existence with your words. You create atmospheres no one can change. When the trials of life appear too much to handle, use this weapon. It is right there in your armory. Use it. Read Isaiah, the Psalms, Jeremiah, Daniel, etc., these all will help you. See what I do. It will open your eyes to see the heavens working on your behalf, instead of being blinded by hell and only able to see the trial or situation that is trying you - so as to work things for your good. Trust Me, not your present circumstances.

February 2

1 Timothy 5:22

Lay hands suddenly on no man, neither be partaker of other men's sins; keep thyself pure. KJV

Ask Me to help you. Don't be so swift to call another your friend or brother. This scripture does refer to leadership, giving leadership to others. Putting your mark of approval on someone when you don't know who they are. Sometimes people will persuade you they are for Christ, when they are nothing of the kind. That they are for your congregation, when they are against it. Be careful of wolves in sheep clothing. When you do this, sometimes you will be a partaker of their sin. That's their motive. As ugly as it sounds, they know exactly what they are doing. Their motive is to trip you up. As they trip you first, the second trip follows, this affects many in your congregation.

Be careful, be still, I am God, ask Me, I will help you with this. Keep yourself pure.

February 3

Proverbs 1:33

But whoso hearkeneth unto me shall dwell safely; and shall be quiet from fear of evil.   KJV

First pay attention to me, and then relax. Now you can take it easy--you're in good hands.

The Message

Busy, busy, busy you are. If you would only stop! Listen to My voice. Take your direction from Me. Servants look to the king at the beginning of their day. The king has the direction the kingdom is going all figured out. When you are off on your own plans you only frustrate your day. By the way, you frustrate others as well. Come here. Speak to Me this morning. I will help you lay out your day. This will flow. And when you lay your head to rest tonight, there will not be all the worries swimming in your head. This My friend, is the peace of God, that which surpasses all understanding.

February 4

Revelation 2:22

Behold, I will cast her into a bed, and them that commit adultery with her into great tribulation, except they repent of their deeds. KJV

Revelation 2:20

But why do you let that Jezebel who calls herself a prophet mislead my dear servants into Cross-denying self-indulging religion?

The Message

Let Me make Myself perfectly clear. There will be a judgment for what goes on on the earth. Except for repentance through Christ, Jesus Christ, there will be no eternity with Me in My heaven. You absolutely must be born again. You absolutely must tell people. I am sovereign, I have designed salvation this way for a reason. Self must be removed from the throne of your life and aspirations. Once the cross is denied, you give hell total access to rule your life. Hell will use your flesh to destroy you and anyone you have influence over. Stay in the Word daily. Speak the Word daily. Put on your weapons daily. You do not fight against flesh and blood. But against the rulers of wickedness in high places. This is spiritual warfare. Pray daily. Put on your armor and prepare for battle if you have any intentions of winning. This is how Christians win. This what is meant by serving God. When I say fight, it will take effort. No war has ever been won without effort. That's not a fight. That would be a rest. I foretold of Christ coming, and of the battle at hand in Isaiah.

Isaiah 59:15-19

(paraphrased) ..And the Lord saw...there was no intercessor; therefore his arm brought salvation ... righteousness ...For he put on righteousness as a breastplate, and an helmet of salvation upon his head; and he put on the garment of vengeance for clothing, and was clad with zeal as a cloak. ... So shall they fear the name of the Lord ... When the enemy shall come in like a flood, the Spirit of the Lord shall lift up a standard against him.

February 5

Proverbs 18:22

He who finds a wife finds a good thing.   KJV

If I tell you a wife is a good thing, then why do you belittle yourself into thinking you have no purpose on earth. Like a quartermaster, you are who maintains and brings supplies to the weary captain. He cannot function correctly without a backup. He is created with the need for a good wife. Many times, it is your encouragement that sets him on the correct path. Many times, it is your love that brings the confidence needed in the hard decisions. All the time it is your meals of self-expression that nourish and guide him throughout his day. How lonely the man without a wife to return to at the end of his day. Her life and smile light up his evenings and bring him the rest so needed from his day. When you care for yourself and stay in prayer with Me; you will be able to meet his needs abundantly. This in turn meets your needs and make it easier for the home to be a place of blessing for all concerned. Go, be fruitful, multiply, love people, do My work, but never dismiss the importance of the role of quartermaster to your husband. It is your lifeline.

February 6

Psalm 61:8

And I'll be the poet who sings your glory -- and live what I sing every day.   The Message

So will I sing praise unto Thy name for ever, that I may daily perform my vows.   KJV

To each of you I give talents. From each of you performing your tasks I receive glory. Never moan at what I have given you to do. Do it well. Always strive to do your best for me.

February 7

Isaiah 65:23

For they themselves are plantings blessed by God, with their children and grandchildren likewise God-blessed.   The Message

When I bring it all together, it will come together. You are a blessed planting. I have called you by name. Fear not and say, "It's too hard. It doesn't look fruitful. This can't be of God". I have set this task before you so that I can use you to complete it. This is the way I do things. As you step out in faith, complete this task one step at a time. One day at a time. The time will come when you will look around in awe at all that I have used you to accomplish on this earth. Your purpose is sure. Your own molding and shaping thru these things is critical. For in the mundane things, the little things, like adding mortar between the bricks builds a great structure, I will build and seal your destiny.

February 8

James 4:8

Draw nigh to God and He will draw nigh to you. Cleanse your hearts, ye double minded. KJV

James 4:10

Humble yourselves in the sight of the Lord, and He shall lift you up. KJV

Get down on your knees before the Master; it's the only way you'll get on your feet.   The Message

When I hear you cry in word and attitude,

"Purify my heart; cleanse me from within; make me holy; I am sorry Lord."

That's when I can move. What will I move to do? I will purify your heart. I will cleanse you. I will make you holy. As I lift you straight up out of the muck and the mire of the sin in your life, you will literally feel it fall off of you and the cleansing of My Spirit will undergird and strengthen you. Walk in the newness and rejoice in your new day. Let Me wipe those tears.

Psalm 46:8

Attention all!!! See the marvels of God! He plants flowers and trees all over the earth.   The Message

Come, behold the works of the Lord, what desolations He hath made in the earth.   KJV

Ahhh! I am the planter. I am the harvester. I sow. I reap. Learn what I teach and your harvest will be overflowing. You want fruitfulness. I hear your cry for it. Here is the key. Sow. Without sowing there will never be a reaping. As a farmer clears the field from all rocks and sticks and anything else he finds while scrutinizing to see what would obstruct his seedlings from maturity, so you must scrutinize your life and remove the obstacles and distractions. If you take care for the field, it brings fertility and nutrition and strength and fruitfulness.

Proverb1:8-9

... Never forget what you learned at your mother's knee. Wear her counsel like flowers in your hair, like rings on your fingers.

The Message

...forsake not the law of thy mother: For they shall be an ornament of grace unto thy head, and chains about thy neck.   KJV

This scripture is about respect for your earthly father as well. I want to remind you of your mother today. No one on earth has bore you from their belly but her. The sacrifices she made took a toll on her throughout her life. When you look back and second guess so many of her decisions and words spoken, also take time to remember she had more going on than you were privy to. Love her because of who she is. I placed you in her womb on purpose. Respect for parents is critical to your growth.

February 11

Acts 18:7

And he departed thence, and entered into a certain man's house, named Justus, one that worshipped God .... KJV

Justus was known to Paul and the believers as a man who worshipped Me. I told Paul, in a vision, to feel free to speak there. The reason Paul could feel free to speak was because he was amongst My people. Many times, you feel unable to speak to others, that is because they are not Mine. Pay close attention to Me. It's great to work with folks, and eat with them, but if they are not saved, and you are not working with them for that purpose of inviting them to know Me, then there will be a clashing of your spirit and theirs. It is critical how you view people. Words are spirit and they make spiritual impact. Strive for their souls, do not be timid. If you cannot strive any longer with them, then walk away. I'll give you wisdom in this.

February 12

Isaiah 46:1-4

Bel boweth down, Nebo stooped, their idols were upon the beasts, and upon the cattle; your carriages were heavy loaded; they are a burden to the weary beast. They stoop, they bow down together; they could not deliver the burden, but themselves are gone into captivity. Hearken unto me, O house of Jacob, and all the remnant of the house of Israel, which are borne by me from the belly, which are carried from the womb. And even to your old age I am he; and even to hoar hairs will I carry you: I have made, and I will bear; even I will carry, and will deliver you.   KJV

Idolatry is ridiculous. I try many ways to show you in My Word. This is one scripture with an illustration of how idolatry is the exact opposite of Me. Idolatry causes you to carry the burden, and makes you weary. I call you to Me, where my burden for you is light, where I carry your burden. I do not cause you weariness, I bring you to rest, to lie down in green pastures. They cannot carry this burden, and they end up in captivity. So as with sin, it leads to captivity. Idolatry is such a perfect picture of sin. It causes weariness. But look at the root of it. Man makes it himself, and insists it's easier than serving Me. Forms it, paints it, gives it fake eyes, fake ears, fake hands, carries it around, pets it, cleans it, and expects it to make them wise, happy and even prosperous. Instead it loads them down and they become weary and bound, ripped off by the lies of hell. Come to Me. I will give you rest.

....I have made, and I will bear; even I will carry, and deliver you.

February 13

Isaiah 26:1-6

.. Steady on their feet, because they keep at it and don't quit. Depend on God and keep at it because in the Lord God you have a sure thing.   The Message

Jesus said, "Many are called, few chosen." This is the reason. Perseverance separates the saints from the aints. It's true. Saints will endure until the end. They work through the rough spots. They have as many of them as you do. Some have much more to bear. Take time for Me. Ask My help. I will never leave you high and dry. The devil is a liar and comes dressed as despair and loneliness. Look up. Your redemption draweth nigh. I'm right here. I am able.

A Wedding Song

Psalms 45

My heart bursts its banks,

spilling beauty and goodness.

I pour it out in a poem to the king,

shaping the river into words:

You're the handsomest of men;

every word from your lips is sheer grace,

And God has blessed you, blessed you so much.

Strap your sword to your side, Warrior!

Accept praise! Accept due honor!

Ride majestically! Ride triumphantly!

Ride on the side of truth!

Ride for the righteous meek!

....God, poured fragrant oil on your head...

Your ozone drenched garments

are fragrant with mountain breeze.

Chamber music - from the throne room -

makes you want to dance

...the Bride glittering with golden jewelry.

Now listen daughter, don't miss a word:

forget your country, put your home behind you.

Be here - the king is wild for you. Since he's your lord, adore him.

Wedding gifts pour in from Tyre..

Her wedding dress is lined with gold.. All her dresses and robes are woven with gold...

She is led to the King...   The Message

You are My bride. Many times, you forget who you are. Hold your head high. You are the bride of a king.

February 15

God is wild for you

Psalms 1:1-2

How well God must like you -- you don't hang out at Sin Saloon, you don't slink along Dead-End Road, you don't go to Smart-Mouth College. Instead you thrill to God's Word, you chew on scripture day and night. The Message

Psalms 1:1-3

Blessed is the man that walketh not in the counsel of the ungodly, nor standeth in the way of sinners, nor sitteth in the seat of the scornful. But his delight is in the law of the Lord; and in his law doth he meditate day and night. And he shall be like a tree planted by the rivers of water, that bringeth forth his fruit in his season; his leaf also shall not wither; and whatsoever he doeth shall prosper. KJV

When you are feeling like there is no fruit in your life. Take time and meditate on this scripture. Check your attitude. Check your routine. Morning and night routines. Line those up with My Word. Read My Word to find out what that would mean. Ask Me. And you shall see that change come and your season will be fruitful beyond measure. I am the Lord of the harvest. I long to bless you. You are mine. And yes, I am wild about you. Let's get to work. Look to see where I am moving. Pray about it. Then move in that direction.

February 16

John 14:26

The Counselor, the Holy Spirit, whom the Father will send in my name, will teach you all things. KJV

When I speak to you, that is My Holy Spirit engaging in your life. When you shrug it off, 'not interested ' in His engagement with you, you shrug off Me. Ask yourself why would you shrug off the Creator and Savior of your life? Ponder that. Then re-engage with Me through repentance. Then be prepared. I want to be involved with you. Trust My leadings. I want you to be familiar with My voice. This comes by obedience. And then recognizing the results as Me. Let Me be your own teacher. Me in you.

February 17

John 7:38

Rivers of living water will brim and spill out of the depths of anyone who believes in Me.. KJV

Do you thirst for more? Are you barren and brittle? Does bitterness rot your roots that you so desperately tried to plant in Me through the years. You need to believe in Me. Stop looking at your circumstances. Believe Me. Had Christ looked around and saw His circumstances in His flesh; hell, death, and the grave would not have been conquered that day. When you take things back into your own hands it becomes a mess. Think of the child playing in the garden. She wants to try her hand at mother's work. How much havoc she will do, especially before the harvest is brought in. The tool in her hand will kill everything the mother has planted, cared for, and loved. So, it is with Me. Just have patience. Allow My tender loving care in your life. Allow Me to nurture you with your morning prayer and reading of My Word. This is where the 'rivers of living water will brim and spill out of the depths of you'. I have so much to do in your life. It really will go easier if you learn and obey. I love you so.

February 18

Romans 15:4

For whatsoever things were written aforetime were written for our learning, that we through patience and comfort of the scriptures might have hope. KJV

Hope is a wonderful thing. Remember Paul wrote, these three, faith, hope and charity. It sets right in between faith and love. Without hope there is no joy. Without hope there is no faith. Hope displays love in a most beautiful way. Many will tell you today, "Just ignore the Old Testament." Please take time to show them this scripture I have shared with you from Romans. The Old Testament is for your learning My nature, My promises fulfilled, and My promises yet to be fulfilled. These are the things that bring you the hope. These things in your bible will bring you the patience and comfort you need to master this world. Hope changes things. Hope changed you. Read My Word today. I spoke it for you. Share it with someone you love. I spoke it for them too.

February 19

Genesis 24:22

And it came to pass, as the camels had done drinking, that the man took a golden earring of half a shekel weight, and two bracelets for her hands of ten shekels weight of gold.. KJV

When Abraham's servant was sent to find a wife for his master's son, he was instructed to find a woman who loved God and willing to uproot and follow a husband who loved God, and follow him anywhere. This is a treasure to be sought indeed. And one worthy of treasures that have been set aside and prepared for her before he ever even discovers or sets eyes on her. Never should a man be stingy with his wife. He is a great source of confidence for her. No one else on earth can fill her with this kind of confidence but him. As Christ supernaturally fills her, of course, the husband is the vehicle he uses on this earth to bless and compliment her life. A husband that purposely withholds gifts from his wife will not find favor with God. Her inner struggles will be his to uncomfortably deal with.

Proverb 18:22 He who finds a wife, finds a good thing, and obtains favor of the Lord. KJV

Ephesians 5:25 Husbands, love your wives, even as Christ also loved the church, and gave himself for it. KJV

February 20

Ephesians 3:1 (paraphrased)

For this cause I Paul, ...the dispensation of the grace of God which was given me ... By revelation he made known unto me the mystery; ..when ye read, ye may understand my knowledge in the mystery of Christ which in other ages was not made known...is now revealed unto his holy apostles and prophets by the Spirit. KJV

When Paul wrote these letters, he wrote them to the church. This was how he communicated the gospel to far away congregants. He discipled men to lead churches. Part of that discipleship is these letters. As you glimpse into the early church instructions from Me to Paul to pastors and the Christians, remember I have given you a pastor, a headship as well. I speak to him. He may deliver my message in a sermon to you, by a phone call to you, through conversation with you, but it is My message nonetheless. He prays for you. Pay attention to your headship. Glean from sermons. Read and read again your notes from those sermons. Ponder them. Think on them. Just because his sermons are not contained in your earthly published books, does not mean they do not come from Me. I tailor My message for you. You are My concern today. Draw close, let My revelations and mysteries be made known to you.

Ephesians 3:18-19 May be able to comprehend with all saints what is the breadth, and length, and depth, and height; and to know the love of Christ, which passeth knowledge, that ye might be filled with all the fullness of God.   KJV

February 21

Genesis 1:11 and God said, let the earth bring forth grass, the herb yielding seed, and the fruit tree yielding fruit, after his kind, whose seed is in itself, upon the earth: and it was so.

Leviticus 26:4 then I will give you rain in due season, and the land shall yield her increase, and the trees of the field shall yield their fruit.

Genesis 26:12 then Isaac sowed in that land, and received in the same year an hundredfold: and the Lord blessed him.

Deuteronomy 28:1-6 and it shall come to pass, --- if --- thou shalt hearken diligently unto the voice of the Lord thy God, to observe and to do all his commandments which I command thee this day, that the Lord thy God will set thee on high above all the nations of the earth.

And all these blessings shall come on thee, and overtake thee, if thou shalt hearken unto the voice of the Lord thy God.

Blessed shalt thou be in the city, and blessed shalt thou be in the field.

Blessed shall be the fruit of thy body, and the fruit of thy ground, and the fruit of thy cattle, the increase of thy kine, and the flocks of thy sheep.

Blessed shall be thy basket and thy store.

Blessed shalt thou be when thou comest in, and blessed shalt thou be when thou goest out.   KJV

You saw that 'if' I placed in Deuteronomy. That's a big if. That if carries a lot of weight. That if carries My promise. You keep your side of the promise and I will keep mine. It has always been that way. Massive fruitfulness, with increase and enlargement. I'm not going to give you a little harvest, but a big harvest. Just listen to me. Do what I tell you to do. Go into all the world and preach the gospel and it's not coming back empty. I am Lord of the harvest, not lord of the barrenness. I'll bring the increase. Wait patiently for the latter rain. The rapture is close. I know you can smell it. Revival is coming. And the hard-working farmer will be first to receive. You need to double down on this. Work hard. What else have I called you for?

Ezekiel 36:30 and I will multiply the fruit of the tree, and the increase of the field, that ye shall receive no more reproach of famine among the heathen.

-----You will never again bear the reproach of famine.   KJV

February 22

Revelation 2:21-28

I am he which searcheth the reins and hearts; ... Hold fast till I come. And he that overcometh and keepeth my works unto the end, to him will I give power over the nations: ... And I will give him the morning star. KJV

You long for a change in your life. The mundane is causing you drowsiness and lethargy. Hold fast child. The breaking is coming. Look again. Look to the left and look to the right. The beginning and the end. I am an overcomer. Remember your reference points of life where I have moved in the past. There are many times when all seems quiet and mundane, however, I must prepare some things before your next victory. Look up. Your redemption draws nigh. Stay in My Word. Keep on the whole armor. Draw close to me if you feel depressed and wanting to break free, when I have instructed you to wait and be patient. Do not wander into the sin of this world. Do not give hell an inch of ground in your life. Do not allow gaps in the armor thru fear or frustration or disobedience. Trust. It is absolutely critical you trust Me during this time. I got this!

February 23

Quick, take cover

Ephesians 6:17 And take the helmet of salvation ... KJV

Your mind - 99.9% of your battle will be fought in the mind. Somewhere you must get the revelation that My salvation, that was won on Calvary's cross, is enough to win that battle. I have given you a powerful tool in life. In the physical it is protected by a hard bone. No part of your body lives life on this earth so well protected. In the spiritual you have a helmet that must be 'put' on. Pull it on. Through prayer of salvation. When you are being attacked, bow and pray. That salvation is sufficient to protect the mind. Hell is real. Hell's assaults are real, and particularly, not haphazardly, put together to destroy you. Hell has no friends. Do not entertain such thoughts. The spirit of this world and in this age roams about. Look at the victories it has claimed all around you. The same tactics are used against you. That is why being in morning prayer, and digging into My Word is critical. It keeps you close to me and firmly sets in place the helmet of salvation. Stay equipped. Stay covered. This fight comes out right for those who actually fight. For those who do not, it will not end so well. Eyes forward, think of heaven.

February 24

1 Corinthians 2:1-2

...I deliberately kept it plain and simple: first Jesus and who he is; then Jesus, and what he did -- Jesus crucified.   The Message

And I, brethren, when I came to you, came not with excellency of speech or wisdom, declaring unto you the testimony of God. For I determined not to know anything among you, save Jesus Christ, and him crucified.   KJV

When I sent My Son, I sent Him for a purpose. If you were the only one on earth that required salvation I would have sent Him anyways. My will is that none should perish, but that all should come to salvation. When I send you to the streets to speak to this one or that one, it is critical you keep it simple.

-Who Jesus is,

  -the Son of God,

  -the only name given under heaven where by you must be saved,

  -the one able and willing to forgive you of your sin, and

  -the one God gave you for salvation because of His love for you.

  -Jesus was crucified and rose from the dead to give you victory over and freedom from your sin and bondages.

Leave the rest to Me.

He's in the still small voice

1 Kings 19:11-12

and he said, Go forth, and stand upon the mount before the Lord. And, behold, the Lord passed by, and a great and strong wind rent the mountains, and brake in pieces the rocks before the Lord; but the Lord was not in the wind; and after the wind an earthquake; but the Lord was not in the earthquake. And after the earthquake a fire; but the Lord was not in the fire; and after the fire a still small voice.   KJV

Take time to be alone with Me. You must take time alone so that you can hear and recognize My voice. How else shall you know when I call? How else shall you know when I warn? How else shall you know when I correct? This is where your protection lies. In hearing and recognizing My voice, and in learning to react as soon as I speak. Come, meet with Me. Shhhh. Listen.

John 10:27-28

My sheep hear My voice, and I know them, and they follow Me. And I give them unto eternal life; and they shall never perish, neither shall any man pluck them out of My Father's hand.   KJV

Numbers 23:19

God is not like people, who lie; He is not a human who changes his mind. Whatever he promises, he does; He speaks, and it is done. GNTD

I will never lie to you. Any misrepresentation is not by Me. Trust Me. Fill your life with My Word. Come to Me in the mornings and let Me refresh you like a morning dew. It's going to be alright. I have things under control. I do not pace in heaven wringing My hands in desperation with nowhere to turn. Your enemy is real and blinds you from Who I Am many times. Look past the enemy and the circumstance. You will see Me. Eyes forward. Think of heaven.

February 27

Psalms 141:3

Set a watch, O Lord, before my mouth; keep the door of my lips. KJV

If you would but ask, I can move. You must guard your tongue. The words you speak create an atmosphere for Me to move, or My hands to be tied. Speak life. Speak healing. Try this: I am believing God to heal this headache - instead of cursing while you look for an aspirin bottle. Try this: God is going to help us, let's pray - instead of, are you kidding, you screwed this up again? Try this: God has this under control, He knows what to do, lets pray, - instead of, I don't know what to do anymore God just doesn't seem to care. Try this: Will you pray for me? Instead of - I am never going back to church, those people don't care about me.

If you will but ask, I can move. If you will but guard your tongue, I can change the world with the love you would be able to show. Would you be My hands and feet today and take time for others, regardless of what you are going through?

February 28

Payday

Are your labors worthy? Do you work hard? Do I have your loyalty as an employer does? Do you show up to work every day? Do you work an honest day for an honest pay? Do you love your work and strive to be the best you can? Do you keep a good appearance and strive to live clean, in the physical and the spiritual? Are you friendly to the other help? Are you helpful to those who come to you to want to know about Me? Are you willing to go the extra mile with a good heart? Are you a good example of Me and Mine?

How much are you worth?

Proverbs 31:10 Who can find a virtuous woman? For her price is far above rubies. KJV

I see your labors. I know you see My Word. I do not neglect Mine. Not on earth nor in heaven. You will be blessed beyond reason. Your rewards are unfathomable. Trust Me. Again, eyes forward. Think of heaven.

February 29

Proverbs 23:13-14

Withhold not correction from the child; for if thou beatest him with the rod, he shall not die. Thou shalt beat him with the rod and shalt deliver his soul from hell. KJV

Don't be afraid to correct your young ones; a spanking won't kill them. A good spanking, in fact, might save them from something worse than death. The Message

Some mothers are very good at 'manipulating' their children into behaving correctly. But you watch and see what I do with the ones that are 'raised correctly'. Discipline goes a long long way. All the way into adulthood, long after the child has left the home and is no longer yours to discipline, your lessons and teaching in love will remain. Hang around a while and watch what I do.

Proverbs 22:6 Train up a child in the way he should go; and when he is old, he will not depart from it. KJV

Point your kids in the right direction-- when they're old they won't be lost. The Message

March 1

1 Corinthians 13

(Read this as if Paul was writing this directly to you- because he is --try reading it out loud with some passion and purpose - because he wrote it that way. You may grasp it more if you think of the word 'love' where he uses 'charity')

Though I speak with the tongues of men and of angels, and have not charity, I am become as sounding brass, or a tinkling cymbal. And though I have the gift of prophecy, and understand all mysteries, and all knowledge; and though I have all faith, so that I could remove mountains, and have not charity, I am nothing. And though I bestow all my goods to feed the poor, and though I give my body to be burned, and I have not charity, it profits me nothing.

Charity suffers long, and is kind; charity envies not; charity vaunts not itself, is not puffed up. Doesn't behave itself unseemly, seeks not her own, is not easily provoked, thinks no evil; rejoices not in iniquity, but rejoices in truth; bears all things, believes all things, hopes all things, endures all things. Charity never fails; but whether there be prophecies, they shall fail; whether there be tongues, they shall cease; whether there be knowledge, it shall vanish away. For we know in part, and we prophesy in part. But when that which is perfect is come, then that which is in part shall be done away.

When I was a child, I spoke as a child, I understood as a child, I thought as a child; but when I became a man, I put away childish things.

For now we see through a glass darkly; but then face to face; now I know in part; but then shall I know even as also I am known. And now abides faith, hope, charity, these three; but the greatest of these is charity.   KJV

The Message Version says the last verse like this:

trust steadily in God, hope unswerving, love extravagantly - until that completeness comes.

When I send My Son back, it will be as a judge. He has already saved the world, sacrificing all. While you wait upon His return, rapture, or your death and appointment at the judgment seat, take time and think on scripture. This one particularly. Because My Son spoke Himself many times about the need for you to love people. Without love you cannot and will not enter heaven. The saving power of Christ gives you victory over hate and malice. Take time to love people. This will be a strength to you. Such a strength that you will not recognize yourself over time. I will be able to use you as a powerful testimony of the saving grace of Jesus Christ. Try this. When they speak ill towards you, look past them, maybe even physically around them, and see Me. I will help you.

March 2

1 Corinthians 1:1

....to them that are sanctified in Christ Jesus, called to be saints KJV

...believers cleaned up by Jesus and set apart for a God-filled life. The Message

Sanctification is not just a salvation miracle, it takes time to clean off the old; and the new to take its place in your life. Don't get Me wrong. Salvation begins the process. At the same time always remember the process is incomplete while in your earthly body and environment. However, sanctification is what I strive for in you. Without it, you miss out on many of the gifts I have for you. So many times, I am unable to bless you because of this very thing. Sanctification is holiness. Jesus spoke to you, "be you holy, as I am holy." Those are powerful words. Those are words that seem unattainable. Many in the world even use them as a 'put down' to you. The many 'holier than thou' statements. But you can be sure I am requiring you to be holy. If I require it, then you very well know that I will mold and shape you into that, with My very own hand. It's the refiner's fire, the trials, the struggles, the hard times, which will mold this in you. Think of an athlete, or even yourself, as the physical body is put through exercise and work outs, the 'padding' or fat or 'unwanted portions' deteriorate and the muscle mass, the desired portion, takes its place. This is no easy task. Much training and work go into this. Pain is what builds the muscle, resistance causes the pain. Without muscle you are left weak. So also for the sanctified, as the sins and desires of this world are burned away, less of your flesh, or unholiness is left, and more of Me, My Holy Spirit will remain. This creates a powerful, sanctified person that I can use in this generation to touch the lost, hurting, and sick. You are called by Me to be a saint, a believer cleaned up by Jesus and set apart for a God-filled life. Grace will carry you, My grace is sufficient.

March 3

1 Corinthians 2:7

God's wisdom is something mysterious that goes deep into the interior of His purposes....   The Message

But we speak the wisdom of God in a mystery, even the hidden wisdom, which God ordained before the world unto our glory; KJV

My longing is to bring out the best in you. To make you and mold you into a powerful disciple and saint of mine. As you draw closer, you see your own flaws more glaringly. However, remember, if you were not drawing close, the flaws would not be so obvious. When you see more of the flaws, it only means you're closer. Come into the light. It is a part of the mystery.

March 4

2 Timothy 1:7

For God hath not given us the spirit of fear; but of power, and of love, and of a sound mind. KJV

I will not give you a Spirit of fear. Fear cripples. Fear paralyzes. Fear not, is what I say, time and time again. Be bold. Take the world for Me. They long for one to stand up and show them an escape route from the life they are caught up in. Remember Satan's chains are very real. His addictions and torments are no light thing. They cannot and will not be broken easily. If you were taken hostage with a friend and found an escape, would you not take the friend with you as you made your way out? Of course, you would. It would be heartless to leave anyone, let alone a friend in bondage while you tasted freedom. Share My gospel of deliverance. Don't be stingy with it. This is why Christ died. Carry on.

March 5

Luke 15:16

..and no man gave unto him. KJV

The prodigal son. What a tremendous picture or illustration of life. When you leave your Father, My protection, My resources, My love, and My will and design for your life; you end up in places you never dreamed of going. Remember he was a very educated Jewish man. He understood the filthiness of the swine. Here he was, reduced to feeding and eating with the pigs. He, like so many, was violating his conscience every day, at the guise of meeting his needs, or putting a roof over his head, or putting food on his table, --- or making the payment on his new vehicle, --- or taking that great vacation --- on and on they go --- these excuses of mankind. When his work was respectable and honest and plenty where he just left. Here he was now, with nothing. In fact, it is summed up in those words, 'no man gave him anything.' People lure you in, and then turn their backs on you when they see, as well as you do, this doesn't work without your Father. Amidst the mundane of life are also the blessings. It is up to you to find the joy in Christ, and appreciate your mundane, protected and filled life. There is nothing out there. The devil and his friends are liars. Trust Me. When you leave Me, you end up with zero folks around to help you.

March 6

Zaccheus

Luke 19:3

And he sought to see Jesus who he was; and could not for the press, because he was little of stature.   KJV

Because Zaccheus was a thief, he had few friends. So, few that in fact in this crowd they would press him out. He couldn't find grace amongst a one of them. Oh, but Christ knew his name. He called up to him and invited Himself into his life. Zaccheus accepted, and his life was never the same. Sin separates. Christ restores. Sin loses friends. Christ is the one who will stay closer than a brother. Zaccheus never had to climb a tree again to get a glimpse of Christ. They spend eternity together only because he accepted the invitation to allow Christ into his life. This is real. Take time to ponder on that miracle of a changed life. Those about you are in the same need. And by the way, many are thieves, but all are sinners.

March 7

Song of Solomon 2:10-11

Get up my dear friend, fair and beautiful lover- come to me! Look around you! Winter is over ... The Message

Yes, the rapture is still coming. Be not weary of well doing. For a day will come when you shall be caught up in the air. Stay working, stay faithful. For it comes at an hour you will not expect, but it will come, as a thief in the night. I will gather Mine home to Me. Do not be left behind. It will not be a situation you would like to find yourself in. Look up. Your redemption draws nigh. And when you

are raptured, the winter will be over, and the spring will last for
eternity.

March 8

Song of Solomon 2:12

*The flowers appear on the earth; the time of the singing of the
birds is come...... KJV*

*Spring flowers are in blossom all over the world. The whole
world's a choir - and singing!   The Message*

Not only does the beauty of new life bring joy to the eye, but also the
ear. Can you find the smell, the aroma anywhere else in a bottle
made by man? They only try to capture it, but oh how they fail. If I
would take so much time to dress the lilies and sprinkle the perfumes
across the fields and bring life and joy to birds that are here today
and gone tomorrow, how lovely can you imagine heaven will be?
The aroma and smells are beyond your comprehension. Breathe in
and try to think on this. The sights, the sounds, all of these also await
you, my bride. Trust Me, follow Me. The road seems hard, and
long, and never ending, just like the winter, but oh, when that spring
breaks forth, and it always does just as I have promised, and the page
turns to hope of warmth and blossoms, the daffodils and the tulips
poke their heads from the ground and bring a smile to your face in
the midst of any trial you may be in. New life is an amazing thing.
Stay faithful my dear, I am right here with you. You have some
growing to do, then you will be home here with Me. Think on
heaven. It will last for eternity.

Psalms 23:6 .....I will dwell in the house of the Lord forever.   KJV

2 Timothy 3:16-17

*All scripture is given by inspiration of God, and is profitable ....
That the man of God may be perfect ...   KJV*

*Every part of Scripture is God-breathed... training us to live God's
way. The Message*

Every verse is inspired by Me. You have My Words, your God, so
that you may know My nature. I bring direction by My Spirit
through the Word. Do not ignore the parts you dislike, and keep the
ones you do like. This causes an imbalance in your walk. You must
allow every scripture to speak to you. Allow it to convict and correct
you. Scripture enables you to discern doctrine. How would you
know unless you know My Word? You will be deceived if you do
not know the Word. This is how you obtain righteousness, which is
being in right standing with Me. The lamp and light of your bible
guides you and makes a way for you to walk. Learn it, then apply it.
Search the scriptures for the answers to give people. Allow the Word
to permeate your life. Share the nuggets you find. Make scriptures a
daily part of your life. Don't let a day go by without Me in your
mornings.

Gideon's Spring

Judges 7:9-12

*That night, God told Gideon: "Get up and go down to the camp.
I've given it to you. If you have any doubts about going down, go
down with Purah your armor bearer; when you hear what they're
saying, you'll be bold and confident." ... The Message*

You will never take victories for Me without obedience. You will
never see breakthrough without Me. If I gave them to you without

'Me' - you - would rush in and take the glory. When you have doubts if it's Me or not, do as I told Gideon: go anyway - then see what I'm doing. Open your eyes, open your ears, not your face down in the water as was the habit of some of Gideon's men. Eyes forward. Ears open. See. Hear. Pay attention to what I am doing. That is giving Me control of your life. When you run, run, run with so many tasks of your own, so many that you rarely take time to see where I am moving, how do you expect that to be blessed with fruitfulness by Me? Relinquish control to Me today, now, and watch what I'm doing. I long to bless your life with a fruitfulness beyond comprehension. Trust Me!

March 11

Isaiah 12:4

And in that day shall ye say, Praise the Lord, call upon his name, declare his doings among the people, make mention that his name is exalted. KJV

In the day of your salvation, from that day forward, a relationship with Me is forged. A unity with Me is established. Growth begins as you draw close to Me. A natural outflow of that is sharing who I am with others. I saved you for a purpose. All roads in every purpose of your life leads to souls. The souls of men and women in your generation that need Christ. Take time for others. I will give you the words to speak. Make mention of My name, declare what I have done for you, ask Me if you struggle with this. I will help you. Trust Me.

Ecclesiastics 1:8-10

...the eye is not satisfied..nor the ear....   ..there is no new thing under the sun. ... Is there any thing whereof it may be said, See this is new? It hath been already of old time, which was before us. KJV

Ah, yes, the mundane. You get so irritated by the mundane. But don't you realize a mundane life of safety and love and security is what so many long for that do not have it. Many days and labors have gone into your foundation to create the mundane life. Do not despise this. This is usually a mark of wisdom. Carry on. Troubles come to all lives. It is the nature of a fallen world and the life of a Christian whom I have called. As your Spirit filled life collides with the world, temptations and trials will come. If not carefully lived - your mundane, safe life will end up in ruins. Just because it looks good on the other side of life, do not be fooled. They long for your life. When trials come to you - I carry and direct you through. Not the sinner, they fall and make a spectacle of it, and resort to trying to fill their emptiness with vacations and partying. They are empty and without a clue. Follow Me. I am the way, the truth and the life. My grace truly is sufficient for you. Heaven is coming. Trust Me.

March 13

Isaiah 43:19

Behold, I will do a new thing; now it shall spring forth; shall ye not know it? I will even make a way in the wilderness, and rivers in the desert. KJV

When you wake in the morning and realize it is not going to be your best day on earth, take time to remember I am able. What am I able to do? Abundantly and above all things. Above all things. Above all things. I am able. When you feel fear and unbelief closing in on you, take time to remember. Those spirits are not of Me. Do not allow them to dictate your actions and responses today. Look to Me. Ask Me for help. I will envelope and direct you. I will guide you through this day. You live and operate and exist in a sinful world. There are many fruits of sin that manifest themselves because of this. The fruit of the sin will affect you by reason of existing and living amongst it. There will be suffering. But I, a righteous God, have chosen prayer; as a vehicle for you to navigate through this world, as a resting place for you when you meet with Me, and as a tool to change things. Prayer is critical for you to know how to react when in seasons of suffering. I will never give you one more test than you can bear. I walk through it with you. Look up, I am here. Be all ears and eyes towards Me.

March 14

John 14:6 I am the way, the truth and the life...KJV

I come to bring you life, and that truly is life more abundantly. You know and believe I am life. You know and believe I shed my blood for you. Yet so many times you forget the power that was established for you through the resurrection. I am able. That now computes out, you are able. Through Me you truly can do all things. Always remember to ask. It is critical to our relationship. Do not allow the spirit of rejection to alter our relationship. Always ask. I will always answer. Contend in prayer. I promise I will always meet you there.

Proverbs 24:10

If you fail under pressure, your strength is too small. NLT

If thou faint in the day of adversity, thou strength is too small. KJV

Good morning. Seize the day. It is yours. No matter what pressures lie ahead, you will be victorious. Let My fruits of My Spirit manifest themselves in you. There is the strength. If you cannot, then you need to fast, pray and contend. I am right here. When you operate in the fruits, your strength will abound. Without them will come failures and frustrations. Pray this way: Father, I pray that you would manifest Yourself in me as patience in this situation.

Gal 5:22-23

But the fruit of the Spirit is love, joy, peace, forbearance, kindness, goodness, faithfulness, gentleness and self-control. Against such things there is no law. NIV

March 16

Philippians 2:5

Let this mind be in you, which was also in Christ Jesus. KJV

You have your carnal mind. I gave you a brilliant brain, it feeds off of your mind and operates and dictates your actions and this in essence is 'you'. It is how you become a shaped character. At salvation, I gave your brain access to My mind. To My Spirit. But your mind is carnal, it is at war with the mind I have given you access to. When your mind makes decisions it actually forms your brain and the way it develops and processes life. Add to that mix the fiery darts of your enemy, the devil, who wants to destroy you. If you will stop and cast out thoughts, cast down fiery darts, I will give you a new mind, filled with Me, your brain will form and be renewed as it processes more and more My way. Walk with Me. Take time to stop and think. Take time to process things through Me. I will help you. This is what will change the thought process. This is what will be your strength instead of your weakness. You'll overcome addictions, bitterness, and past torments. I will bring you rest.

March 17

1 Peter 1:16

Be ye holy; for I am holy. KJV

I am fully aware you cannot attain holiness on your own. Did I not create you? Have I not witnessed the fall in the garden which has bled into and corrupted your very nature? Yet I still call you to holiness. When you have access to the 'mind of Christ' you have access to it. Put on the armor. Ask for the renewing of your mind through Christ Jesus. Abstain sinful desires. The Hollywood world wants that to seem prudish. It is not prudish. It is wisdom. Put on My whole armor. It's spiritual, and yours for the asking. I have called you, so I shall equip you. Taste and see that I am good.

March 18

Genesis 2:18

And the Lord God said, it is not good that the man should be alone; I will make him an help meet for him. KJV

My design in your marriage is completion not competition. When I said I would make man a 'help meet' I meant a woman who would complete him. A help that is good enough, ample enough for him. When I designed him, I designed him to need the help. In the perfect world of the garden she wanted to help. On the other side of the garden the roles have become confused. So much so today that there is even a gender confusion on who does what, which has led to gender confusion across the range and scope of everything in the earth. Sin has run so rampant in this arena it has caused more chaos than any one human could comprehend.

Bring completion back into your marriage. Find your biblical role as a wife. Become a help to your husband. Do not ridicule and make a big thing of his errors and flaws. Love him like he is, submit to his headship. Then you will find rest and completion in your role as woman. Then you can prosper and grow. These confusions have hindered your growth. Walk in My design. Make it a goal for 6 months. Mark your calendar. Then turn around and look back and see all I have done. See all you have grown. Trust Me in this.

March 19

Character Change

Genesis 32:24-28

And Jacob was left alone; and there wrestled a man with him until the breaking of the day. And when he saw that he prevailed not against him, he touched the hollow of his thigh; and the hollow of Jacob's thigh was out of joint, as he wrestled him. And he said, Let me go, for the day breaketh. And he said, I will not let thee go, except thou bless me. And he said unto him, What is thy name? And he said, Jacob. And he said Thy name shall be called no more Jacob, but Israel; for as a prince hast thou power with God and with men, and hast prevailed.   KJV

I know you want power. I know you want blessing. But there are character flaws in your life which hinder you. When I asked Jacob his name, it was not because I didn't know it. I asked him because he didn't know it. Jacob means thief, deceiver, swindler, schemer. He was all of these things. Jacob was in desperate need of a character change. I had to get him alone, and deal with him. With Jacob I had to literally wrestle him and he fought so hard he hurt himself. You cannot wrestle with Me and win. But he did wrestle. He took the time because he wanted that blessing. And he got it. And he got My power besides. But not before I showed him who he was. You know when he spoke his name to Me, he was actually astonished and whispered it with great passion. The repentance flowed from his heart. Will you allow Me, to get you alone, and reveal to you - your name - what your character flaws are - that hinder Me from blessing you and releasing My power into your life. I am not trying to hurt you, nor inflict pain on you. I want to help you. I want to change you from your old sinful nature. Your name is powerful, that new one I have for you - I want to use it in the old one's place. Take time for morning prayer.

March 20

Acts 22:13

.... Brother Saul, receive thy sight. And the same hour I looked upon him. KJV

Healings. These display My power and abilities. How heaven rejoices when we see healings. Always remember to pray for the sick. If they do not get better bring them to church. There is power in your altar call. If you sit with someone who is ill, it is a sad state of affairs that you are too prideful to ask if they would like prayer. Lay hands on them and they will recover. You are My hands on the earth. They hurt, they are miserable, they long for prayer. Please share that with them. Many have come to know me through prayer for sickness and deliverance.

March 21

Acts 2:40

(Peter) He went on in this vein for a long time, urging them over and over, "Get out while you can; get out of this sick and stupid culture!" The Message

Peter had the fire of the Holy Spirit. My Spirit. Straight from the throne. Do you? Do you ever display it? 3,000 got saved that day. 3,000 souls rocked their generation because one man decided to display the power of My Spirit. He wanted to be used by Me. He was not a robot, but a human who decided to see what I would do if he opened his mouth for Me. I can use you. You must be willing to stand up and be used. Trust Me. You want radical converts? Operate in the Spirit. You want rapid growth? Pray out loud. Preach out loud. Speak up and be heard. Quit mumbling. Come out from behind timidity which is just pride anyways. Trust Me!

March 22

God Has a Plan

John 15:15

No longer do I call you servants, for a servant does not know what his master is doing; but I have called you friends, for all things that I heard from My Father I have made known to you. NKJV

I have called you friend. There is a reason for that. I created you for fellowship with Me. That was and still is the reason for man's existence. I long to fellowship with you first thing in the mornings. To start your day with Me on your mind and in your heart. How would a servant begin the day without knowing the requirements of the master that day? I not only lay out the day for you with tasks to be done - I reveal the master's plan. Souls souls souls. It is all about souls. You are in a warfare. Never ever forget that. Look about you. Watch where I am moving. Move with Me. Join Me. For such a time as this you have been brought into the kingdom. And I will mold and shape you into royalty in the process.

March 23

Isaiah 3:5

....the child shall behave himself proudly against the ancient, and the base against the honorable. KJV

Look about you my dear. You are not seeing a generation that generally longs to please me. You look upon a generation that longs to please self. As I have showed you in glimpses through my servant and prophet Isaiah; a generation that seeks 'self-importance', runs way off course. Even those that claim to know Me are so lost they do not recognize it. The outflow is many things. This is one example, the children coming against the elders, thinking themselves wiser than their parents. The pride is seeded so deeply in the adults it is bred into the children. However, it, the spirit of pride, turns on the adults as a worse curse then they could have imagined. They give control of even their own sanity and health to the children. Make no mistake, neither is wise, the child nor the adult. The blindness will overthrow the generation until they return to Me. Sin takes them places they never imagined nor desired to go. Chaos across the earth ensues.

Isaiah 2:5

O house of Jacob, come ye, and let us walk in the light of the Lord. KJV

I long to help you return to the light. Come close to Me. Repent daily. Search and study your own heart through My Word. Let Me in to change you. As you walk with Me you will see things more clearly. Life comes through Christ. This is why He is called the light of the world. You will need Christ to see clearly to be molded and shaped for eternity. Trust Me as I prepare you for heaven. It is going to be a wild ride. Just trust Me and enjoy it. I am right here with you. No need to fear. I got this.

March 25

Isaiah 19:16

In that day shall Egypt be like unto women; and it shall be afraid and fear because of the shaking of the hand of the Lord of hosts, which he shaketh over it. KJV

Do not deceive yourself into thinking that I do not bring warnings and judgments on this earth. Long before the judgment seat in heaven will men experience the shaking of My hand. These 'men' of Egypt became so frightened I called them sissys. Girls. School girls. In your life you have felt My Spirit convict you and tug on you. In your life you have experienced My shaking. These are not because I 'do not' love you, but as a Father disciplines the child he loves and longs to mold and shape, so much more do I love you. I mold and shape you for eternity. Far beyond any mortal father can see. Also, as the child that struggles in his father's discipline and makes his punishment far worse because of it, so is yours with Me.

You pray constantly 'God use me. God change me. God help me be different.' Try this. Do what I ask, when I ask. This is your reasonable service. Turn around in three months and you will not recognize yourself. This is called maturity and growth. Walk with Me. I long to teach you.

March 26

Isaiah 10:10

..and his rest shall be glorious   KJV

The world seeks after a rest. How many times a day do you hear the sighs and longings for rest and peace. The frustrations of sin take their toll on people. You must remind them, always, that the only rest worth having comes from Christ. He is their rest, their thirst quencher, their infilling for the empty heart. Always remember to remind them. When you seem to be going through a season of dryness, unfruitfulness, take a good long drink of the living water. You truly will never thirst again.

Isaiah 12:3 Therefore with joy shall ye draw water out of the wells of salvation.   KJV

March 27

Isaiah 8:1

Moreover, the Lord said unto me, Take thee a great roll, and write in it with a man's pen .....   KJV

When I ask you to do something as simple as record what I have spoken to you, I have a reason for it. Many a morning will I speak these simple tasks into your spirit. This scripture was written very long ago so that My people, including you, today would realize that I spoke to Isaiah the exact same way I speak to you. As you read My Word, keep this in mind. Follow Me. Through the Word, through My promptings to you as well. Trust My voice. I truly am the same yesterday, today and forever. Taking the time to listen to others is many times just what I have for you today. So many times, your friend only needs a listening ear, so as to speak something out loud as I minister to her spirit. Be My faithful servant on earth so that I can change lives through you. Be My hands and feet, and sometimes just my ears. Be still and know that I am God.

March 28

Isaiah 12:2

Behold, God is my salvation; I will trust, and not be afraid; for the Lord JEHOVAH is my strength and my song; he also is become my salvation. KJV

When you enter the covenant with Me you will find My strength. The fruit of My strength is salvation of course, and also with it comes a song of joy in your heart. The devil lurks about seeking to destroy your fruit of joy. When you feel dismayed, like all of life is not seeming to work out how 'you' have planned, take a good look at My plans, through the Word of God. Soak in it daily. As your vision is turned towards Me, your strength and joy will return. Trust in Me, not in feelings. Your flesh will succumb many times. Reign it in through the Word of God. I will bring that song right back in your heart where I planned for it to be since the day you were conceived in your mother's womb. Remember, always remember, I formed you and placed you there, that womb, for a purpose. Never lose sight of that.

March 29

Isaiah 16:2

For it shall be, that, as a wandering bird cast out of the nest, so the daughters of Moab shall be at the fords of Arnon. KJV

A nest forsaken. When Mine have forsaken Me, they become lost. They cannot find their way back because sin causes confusion and chaos. There is no path home, or back to the safety of their nest, without Me. When repentance is sincere it opens the eye, blindness is healed. Paul found this to be so when he was on his way to Damascus. He wanted to serve Me. He wanted to please Me. But he had gotten so off track. Why? Because he refused to acknowledge the saving grace of Jesus Christ. Sin kills. Sin confuses. Sin confounds. Salvation rescues. Salvation brings light. Salvation restores the safety, rebuilds the nest. Come to Me, any that are heavy laden, blind, confused, deaf, unable to cope, I will give you rest. Remember to tell someone these things today.

March 30

Isaiah 6:1-4

..I saw also the Lord sitting upon a throne, high and lifted up, and his train filled the temple. Above it stood the seraphims; each one had six wings; with twain he covered his face, and with twain he covered his feet, and with twain he did fly. And one cried unto another, and said, Holy, holy, holy, is the Lord of hosts: the whole earth is full of his glory. And the posts of the door moved at the voice of him that cried, and the house was filled with smoke. KJV

Revelation 4:11-12

And I beheld, and I heard the voice of many angels round about the throne...thousands and thousands ... Saying with a loud voice, Worthy is the Lamb.... KJV

Jesus paid the price. We have done everything possible in a plan of salvation for your soul. Repent and be baptized. Grow in My Word. Join us in heaven. This is eternity. This is forever. Look not to the right or the left. Keep calm and look towards heaven. Surrender. All your sins are washed away. Everything becomes new.

March 31

Psalms 18:1

I love you, God - you make me strong. God is bedrock under my feet, the castle in which I live, my rescuing knight. My God - the high crag where I run for dear life, hiding behind the boulders, safe in the granite hideout.   The Message

When you draw close to Me in prayer, especially that morning prayer, the first fruits of your day, I will envelope and protect you. How can I be ever so much present unless you meet with Me in the mornings to establish that presence? As you dress for the day for protection against the weather and elements, preparing for battle, or a day at the office, or a day with the children and housework, or simple leisure, so you must put on the garment of praise and repentance to draw close and under My wings. Think spiritually. Live spiritually. Never let anyone dissuade you from the truth of your spiritual existence. The world will come against you. Satan will come against you. Your flesh will fight with both fists many times. Never allow victory to anyone other than My Spirit. Meet with Me. I will move mountains and keep you.

April 1

Isaiah 26:4

Trust ye in the Lord for ever; for in the Lord JEHOVAH is everlasting strength. KJV

Bodily exercise profits little. Your spiritual well-being is at stake. You want to flex muscle, gain protein, grow strong? All of these things may make a fleshly body fit. However, your primary responsibility is the spiritual. How can a fit body that dies and is buried, be of everlasting use to Me?

Keep your eyes on the real prize. Take time for My Word, for your prayer life, for Me, and also for them, the lost. It is all about the souls of men and women of your generation. Be about your Father's business. Do not live foolishly. Look up, live wisely.

April 2

Psalms 120:1

In my distress I cried to the Lord, and he heard me. KJV

Yours is coming. It's right there. You won't receive many words from me because of the ones I send to speak to you. You are thinking where is mine? Why don't I get one? But yours is right there. Blessings I speak of. Answers to your prayers regarding your family. Salvation issues with the ones you love, the ones you contend for daily, have come up before Me. I hear you. Carry on in the work and plans I set before you each day. Your blessings are within a hands grasp. Continue to walk in trusting Me.

April 3

Isaiah 26:20

Come, my people, enter thou into thy chambers, and shut thy doors about thee; hide thyself as it were for a little moment, until the indignation be over past. KJV

When you go through things, there is a hiding place, a covering of Mine, that only Mine can find. Come to Me. Into My chambers. I will cover you. In any calamity, in any tragedy, in any confusion, in any chaos, any conflict, in any temptation, in any sickness, in any distraughtness of soul, in any heartache, in any hurt, in any frustration, I am right here. Do not allow condemnation to separate you from Me. When you feel convicted, repent and come to Me. I am here. I gave My life on that cross, My blood was spilt, for such a time as this. I am right here. I will cover you until the trial passes.

This is growth. When you know and realize your need of Me and My covering and not only have knowledge of it, you will act upon it and understand how to find that covering. Morning prayer is critical. Always always meet with Me before your day begins.

April 4

Isaiah 43:5-6

Fear not; for I am with thee; I will bring thy seed from the east, and gather thee from the west; I will say to the north, Give up; and to the south, Keep not back; bring my sons from far, and my daughters from the ends of the earth. KJV

Note this as you read this; fear is what frustrates the seed being brought to fruition. Fear is a powerful force in the demonic realm. Isolation is as well. Every warring army knows that isolation breeds fear and fear will bring them victory over the target. Fear is a spirit. It is not of Me. It is your enemy. Fear cripples and paralyzes. Fight fear with reminders that I am with you. Trust Me impeccably in every single area of your life. This creates the atmosphere where I can move. When fear moves in on you, look up and pray. Bind and cast out the spirit of fear. Put on a garment of praise for the spirit of heaviness. I will move. Trust Me.

April 5

Isaiah 49:15-16

Can a woman forget her sucking child, that she should not have compassion on the son of her womb? yea, they may forget, yet will I not forget thee. Behold, I have graven thee upon the palms of my hands; thy walls are continually before me. KJV

Isaiah 49:23 .... No one who hopes in me ever regrets it.

The Message

I watch you daily. You meet with Me in the mornings and I speak to your heart. I guide you through your day. As you obey, I mold and shape. When you disobey, I bring the conviction to get you back on track. You have been forged in the fire. You have been heated, and the dross comes to the top. I remove the dross and meet with you again tomorrow morning. As you rest in the evenings I am there with you. As you prepare your meals I am there. Do you see Me in your times of bountifulness? Do you see Me make something out of nothing in your times of famine? Do you hear Me when you are in a season of sorrow and loss? Do you hear Me rejoice and sing over you when you worship and praise? Your walls truly are always before Me. Many days there are those that tear them down. More days are there that you are working diligently to rebuild. Your perseverance shall bring you into the blessing. Look up, look around, it's coming together. I have control of your life. The more you depend on Me the faster the building. Carry on. Think of heaven. My love for you is more immense than your heart can imagine. Carry on. Think of heaven.

April 6

Isaiah 60:22

A little one shall become a thousand, and a small one a strong nation; I the Lord will hasten it in his time. KJV

My timing is everything. Many times, in scripture I must refer to waiting on Me. Trusting Me. That is because: I have a plan! You must be mature enough to wait. You must learn patience. You must pray for My patience to be manifested in you. I have a plan. It involves you. It is the most amazing life you have ever heard of. Your destiny is phenomenal. Your rewards are phenomenal. Here on earth as well as in heaven. Take your eyes off of self. Meet with Me this morning. Let Me give you just a taste of My presence. Wait on Me. And I will fill you. Allow Me to make you a great nation, use you to become the thousand.

April 7

Isaiah 62:4

..thou shalt be called Hephzibah, and thy land Beulah; for the Lord delighteth in thee ... KJV

Yea I would even say unto you today, this beautiful beginning of spring: new beginnings are a specialty of Mine. I glory in them. Even as I turn this page upon the earth, from barrenness and lethargy to the fresh grass and newness of life, so will I even change you. Stop and smell. Stop and see. Take in the brightness of the sun. Enjoy the freshness of each spring rain. See the growth burst forth from the earth? So, shall you and your congregation grow. For I have seen the sacrifice. Am I blind that I do not see? Am I deaf that I do not hear? For yes, I do see, yes, I do hear, and a blessing of fruitfulness such that your congregation nor city has ever experienced is yours. It is within a hands grasp. Trust Me. Let it be so.

April 8

Jeremiah 2:27-29

Saying to a stock, Thou art my father; and to a stone, Thou hast brought me forth; for they have turned their back unto me, and not their face: but in the time of their trouble they will say, Arise and save us. But where are thy gods that thou hast made thee? ..... Wherefore will you plead with me?

Jeremiah 3:9

And it came to pass through the lightness of her whoredom, that she defiled the land, and committed adultery with stones and with stocks.

Jeremiah 3:1

They say, if a man put away his wife, and she go from him, and become another man's, shall he return to her again? shall not that land be greatly polluted? but thou hast played the harlot with many lovers; yet return again to me, saith the Lord. KJV

When you walk away from Me, you will live in a whole different culture. Where I had carried and covered you, you now walk alone amongst wolves looking to destroy you. Don't be deceived into thinking that you can take the fire and lusts of this world and not be burned. Don't even begin to believe that you can afford the price it will cost you. When you were Mine, you were covered. When you are backslidden, you become the world's. You cannot serve two masters. It does not work out that way. People who continually backslide are people who are double minded. They are unstable. None of their ways work out. To become stable, you must learn to repent daily. Remove the idols from your life. Quit flirting with them. In the end they will destroy you.

April 9

Proverbs 25:16

Do you like honey? Don't eat too much, or it will make you sick. NLT

When you get everything you want, the world calls it spoiled, usually referring to a child. I have news for you. Many adults act like children who are constantly indulged. When some things may take time, the adult has no use for the authority who tells them to wait. This is where the most danger comes from when there is too much honey. I expect more than that of you. Be content where I have placed you. Be content with what I have placed in your hands. Your answer to prayer and intercession is within a hand-grasp. Just hold on. Don't give place to the devil or allow him to use discontentment as a wedge into your life.

April 10

Jeremiah 2:32

Can a maid forget her ornaments, or a bride her attire? yet my people have forgotten me days without number. KJV

How does the created snub their nose at the creator? How do they ever come to a place that they believe themselves to be wiser than the one who molded and shaped them in the palm of His hand and placed them in their own mother's womb? Their hearts become cold as they walk deeper and deeper into sin. Their hearts become stone hard the more their rebellion and sin wraps its tentacles about them. This all breeds contempt for Christ, their Creator, which breeds ignorance. Ignoring the truth. Believing the lie. Tread carefully when you start to believe you are wiser than anyone else. Let the warning signs caution you when you lean towards believing your own parents have no wisdom and your new generation and ideas are much more desirable. Fall on your face when you begin to question the ways of your Creator. You need to repent. Some go off, and never return.

Proverbs 8:17

I love them that love me; and those that seek me early shall find me. The Message

When you question every timing of My answer to your prayers it casts doubt on your trust in Me. Lack of trust is unbelief. Unbelief is sin. I know you are human. I know you have flaws. I know you want things quickly, as a weeping child in a market who misunderstands the 'why' behind the 'no'. I expect you to be more mature than that. Eyes up. Look at Me. I am your authority. Trust Me. Seek Me in morning prayer. I will give you confidence. I always always always hear your prayer. Trust Me with the response in the timing needed to attain it correctly.

April 12

Romans 12:8

If you work with the disadvantaged, don't let yourself get irritated or depressed by them. Keep a smile on your face.   KJV

Ah, My greatest rewards are for those that assist those that can never repay on earth. Giving without expecting a big pay day. What a pure heart that is. When you do this, you store up your rewards in heaven. Those rewards are unfathomable. Your brain, your mind, cannot imagine because you have never been to My heaven. Trust Me on this. When all else fails, I am still in control. I got this. Your being My hands and feet changes the course of the person you are assisting. It's all about them.

Romans 12:9

Love from the center of who you are; don't fake it. **The Message**

There truly are snakes in the grass. Sheep in wolves clothing. Don't be them. Put your eyes on those that are open to the gospel. You be you. Let Me use you. Love from your core. That's who I've made you to be. Engage with them. Speak words to edify and encourage. Build their strength with your words. Build your strength with Mine. Stay with Me in the morning prayer, morning readings. As I build you, you turn and build others. It's a flow through. A powerful revelation of My nature.

April 14

John 13:21

When Jesus had thus said, he was troubled in spirit, and testified and said, Verily, verily, I say unto you, that one of you shall betray me. **KJV**

When I walked the earth, I had much trouble in spirit. This act of betrayal was particularly troubling and John knew it. That is why he recorded it as such. A man I had served, ate with, washed his feet, laughed with, fellowshipped with, made plans with, he allowed Satan to enter into his heart and betrayed me for a few dollars. Men have sold me out time and again for much less, some for much more. The troubling in my spirit is for them, however. When Satan entered Judas' life, his heart and soul were lost forever. Many believe they can return whenever, wherever, they please because of My willingness to forgive. The problem with this fallacy is when you sell out to Satan, there is a price tag with that. You give him dominion over all areas of your life. Many do return. Most do not. Do not walk so close to the edge of salvation, toying with and eyeing up sin as something precious to behold. Do not covet the sinner's belongings and positions and lives. You open doors you may never shut. Stay close to Me. In My Word. With My covering. This is what the power of the resurrection is all about. You can say no to sin and live for Me, because I was crucified and rose again.

April 15

Luke 16:8

And the lord commended the unjust steward, because he had done wisely; for the children of this world are in their generation wiser than the children of light.   KJV

Two different peoples, two different goals.

Children of this world know there is a time when they can no longer toil and work. When the body will fail them. So, they put up for those times, they make friends for those times, so that their needs will be met. This is all they have to look forward to, yet they try to make it as comfortable as possible.

Children of light should also know that the time comes when their physical body will fail them and they no longer will work and toil. They should be wise enough to invest in the kingdom of God. This is where the treasure is to be laid up, where moth nor rust can destroy it. This is where their mansion will be prepared and set aside for them. Eternity is forever and it is real. It is within a hands grasp. Look forward to it with joy as you invest in others as well.

April 16

John 20:11

But Mary stood without at the sepulchre weeping; and as she wept, she stooped down, and looked into the sepulchre, and seeth two angels in white sitting, the one at the head, and the other at the feet, where the body of Jesus had lain. And they say unto her, Woman, why weepest thou? She saith unto them, Because they have taken away my Lord, and I know not where they have laid him. And when she had thus said, she turned herself back, and saw Jesus standing, and knew not that it was Jesus. Jesus saith unto her, Woman, why weepest thou? Whom seekest thou? KJV

Mary did seek Me. When others didn't, Mary came. That's why she found Me. Only those who seek will find. Take time to seek Me and My will. I will rock and shake the very foundations of your world and belief system if you will but seek to find. Push through the mundane and press for the high calling. You want to know the difference between those who press and those who do not? I tell you it is knowledge, but it is also the true joy, the joy unspeakable. Press on. Trust Me. I will fulfill promises made, that even like Mary, you didn't understand the magnitude of the promise, nor realize the power that will befall you when the promise is fulfilled.

April 17

John 3:16

For God so loved the world, that he gave his only begotten Son, that whosoever believe in him should not perish, but have everlasting life. KJV

Take time to reflect and remember who the risen Lord is. This is the season, the time when the resurrection power was released into the earth. The newness of life, the spring, yes it carries with it much of the same spirit. But oh, the power of the resurrection is far beyond anything your human mind can comprehend. Rest in it, rise in it, operate in it, pray in it, live in it, joy in it, be free in it. Power that is tapped into from on high, it is nothing like the world can ever grasp nor duplicate.

April 18

1 John 3:1-3

Behold, what manner of love the Father has bestowed upon us, that we should be called the sons of God; ...we shall be like him ... every man that hath this hope in him purifies himself, even as he is pure. KJV

Do not be disillusioned when going through times of testing and fiery trials. Disappointments and disillusionments always follow a disciplined life. It's part of faith. Will you trust Me even when it's not looking so good for you? These times build your faith. Do not fear. Fear breeds unbelief. Just eyes forward, think of heaven. I got this. Trust Me. Carry on. Witness to the lost. Share My gospel. It's all for the growth of the Christian and also for the kingdom, but mostly for the lost. Look up, My redemption draws nigh.

April 19

Jeremiah 15:20-21

And I will make thee unto this people a fenced brasen wall; and they shall fight against thee, but they shall not prevail against thee; for I am with thee to save thee and to deliver thee, saith the Lord. And I will deliver thee out of the hand of the wicked, and I will redeem thee out of the hand of the terrible. KJV

When you feel the resistance to what you know is My will, pray. I have formed you for such a time as this. Spiritual warfare is a war. You must learn to combat it in the spiritual. When you allow these circumstances, created by the enemy, to affect your relationship with Me, to affect your walk with Me, to affect your witness and testimony for Me, you are giving ground to hell. When you pray you give me the opportunity to make you a brazen wall before your enemy. This in fact is where your deliverance and safety will come from. Your prayer life is critical. Take time. Do not put it off. Does a soldier forget to dress for the day in his uniform and armor? No! And nor should you. Would a soldier decide to take a day off in the midst of incoming mortar attacks? Absolutely not! And nor should you. Put on your armor today. Stand tall in My presence. In the midst of onslaught of doubt and disillusionment, stand. Stand very tall, in Christ!

April 20

Jeremiah 17:5-6

Thus saith the Lord; Cursed be that man that trusteth in man, and maketh flesh his arm, and whose heart departeth from the Lord. For he shall be like the heath in the desert, and shall not see when good cometh; but shall inhabit the parched places in the wilderness, in a salt land and not inhabited. KJV

Jeremiah 17:7-8

Blessed is the man that trusteth in the Lord, and whose hope the Lord is. For he shall be as a tree planted by the waters, and that spreadeth out her roots by the river, and shall not see when heat cometh, but her leaf shall be green; and shall not be careful in the year of drought, neither shall cease from yielding fruit. KJV

Come to Me all who labor and are heavy burdened. I long to give you rest. I am the one that gives the soul rest. I am the place where the lost and hurting are restored. I am the one who died and rose again that you might live. Trust in Me. I long to bless you. Resurrection power and strength restores the weary and faint hearted. Life more abundantly is My natural outflow. Enter My courts through praise and a repentive heart, you shall return in fruitfulness and everlasting joy. Are you thirsty? Drink of Me. Are you hungry? Sit with Me and eat My Word as a daily portion. It will fill you beyond imagination or expectation.

April 21

Jeremiah 22:13-16

Woe unto him that buildeth his house by unrighteousness, and his chambers by wrong; that useth his neighbour's service without wages, and giveth him not for his work; That saith, I will build me a wide house and large chambers, and cutteth him out windows; and it is cieled with cedar, and painted with vermilion. Shalt thou reign, because thou closest thyself in cedar? did not thy father eat and drink, and do judgment and justice, and then it was well with him? He judged the cause of the poor and needy; then it was well with him: was not this to know me? saith the Lord. KJV

When you build your home on the backs of others, you will pay a price. You may believe you are increasing yourself by hiring cheap labor or employing those you can use and not pay a fair price. However, the price you pay spiritually for that is far beyond what you know. When you do these things, not appreciate the labors of others for your benefit, you do yourself and yours a great disservice. I will not honor that home nor its inhabitants. Be generous. Be gracious. Those are the fruits of the spirit. I can bless those. Then, and only then, I can take what you have and bless it far beyond reason. This is a spiritual walk, not a mathematical equation. Come out of the physical. Bless others, especially those you have labor for you. Build a home, but remember there are other needs about you besides just your home. What good does it do you to have a nice home, surrounded and comforted while neglecting the things of the kingdom. Find the balance. Listen to My voice. I will teach you.

I take only the good

Proverbs 21:22

A wise man scaleth the city of the mighty, and casteth down the strength of the confidence thereof. KJV

I look for such a one as this. The one who can take on cities. The one who is constantly looking and alert for new battles to be won. However, when they fight, they fight with wisdom. These are the ones I set apart, some say, single out. What other ones could I possibly use then these? If there are no risks, there are no victories. If there are no costs, there are no gains. When you feel it's too strenuous, ask Me for the strength. Don't weary, press on through discipline. How will you teach and train if I cannot teach and train you? It must come thru fiery trials and testing. You sacrificed. Trust Me to come through where you need Me.

Let God Bring the Fire

1 Kings 18:37-38

Hear me, O Lord, hear me, that this people may know that thou art the Lord God, and that thou hast turned their heart back again. Then the fire of the Lord fell, and consumed the burnt sacrifice, and the wood, and the stones, and the dust, and licked up the water that was in the trench. KJV

I accomplished My purpose through Elijah's obedience. You might be building the altar, bringing the people, taking care of all kinds of things. But, only I bring the fire. And I only will bring the fire through obedience. Is there anything in your life you are attempting to do, that if I don't help you, it won't happen? If you only do what you have confidence you can do without Me, then where am I in this equation? Step out in faith. When I call you to a task, run with it. Do not doubt. I will teach and anoint. I will bring the tasks I have called you to, to completion. I bring the fire. Where's the victory if you can do it yourself? What's even the point? Take time to look around. If you don't have lasting fruit, maybe you're doing it yourself. Some say, "Don't just stand there, do something." I say, "Don't just do something, stand still, wait on Me." Build your relationship with Me, right where you are at. Experience Me first. So, I can use you in Kingdom purposes. I want to accomplish My will through you. Will you be My servant? Will you find out what's on My heart? Will you be involved with what I am doing? If anyone serves Jesus, the Father will honor it.

1 Kings 18:39

And when all the people saw it, they fell on their faces; and they said, The Lord, he is the God; the Lord, he is the God.   KJV

April 24

Contentment

1 Timothy 6:6-9

But godliness with contentment is great gain. For we brought nothing into this world, and it is certain we can carry nothing out. And having food and raiment let us be there with content. But they that be rich fall into temptation and a snare, and into many foolish

and hurtful lusts, which drown men in destruction and perdition.
KJV

You are required to be clay in the potter's hand. You are being
molded and shaped by the Master. How can I mold a hard heart?
You must be pliable. I can only use a contented heart. A heart filled
with Me. Trust Me. I can mold you. Resist, and you are not fit for
My use. I cannot use you. People who chase money will find it.
That's why they have it. Many times, you do not because that is not
the center of your life. Be content with Me. I am your provider. Do
not feel condemned when you don't have as 'much' as them. I see it
differently. You have much more. However, you must chase Me
instead of worldly pleasures. You must in order to have fruit for My
kingdom that will remain.

1 Timothy 6:10-13

For the love of money is the root of all evil; which while some
coveted after, they have erred from the faith, and pierced
themselves through with many sorrows. But thou, O man of God,
flee these things; and follow after righteousness, godliness, faith,
love, patience, meekness. Fight the good fight of faith, lay hold on
eternal life, whereunto thou art also called, and hast professed a
good profession before many witnesses. KJV

April 25

Hebrews 10:23

Let us hold fast the profession of our faith without wavering; for
he is faithful that promised. KJV

Because I have called you to this and set you in this place, you know
that I am helping you. Have I not blessed you along the way? Have I

not even blessed your children with spouses and children and lands and homes? Did you not lay hands upon them when they were young and pray for those spouses in particular? Am I not faithful and able? Did you not pray for your grandchildren even before they were conceived? Trust Me. They must come to their own relationship with Me. I am able to do that. I have blessed you beyond measure. When I look at you I see faithfulness. You are covered in the blood of Christ, this is what I see. You can lean on Me in your struggle and make it through this recent trial. Trust Me.

April 26

Jeremiah 42:11

Be not afraid of the King of Babylon, of whom you are afraid; be not afraid of him, saith the Lord: for I am with you to save you, and to deliver you from his hand. KJV

When you walk in fear, it stays My hand. It stops Me. When you walk in trust, I am able. I am able to save and deliver you. Repent of fear, it is a spirit and a trap set against your life. Repentance is key to overcoming this spirit. You will not overcome it without repentance. Then look forward, carry on, and see Me right on the other side of the situation. Carry on today as if the circumstance was already overcome, because it is. Put a smile on your face, the outward joy on display, to know the inward joy. I am in control. Trust Me.

April 27

Jeremiah 42:3

That the Lord thy God may shew us the way wherein we may walk, and the thing that we may do. KJV

Many have asked, "What would you have me do Lord?" And then they don't believe the answer. Too high a price they think. As you get to know My voice, take time to obey it. It will sound more and more familiar. In the difficult times, very often, it is a difficult way out. But My ways are never your ways. So, take My way out. Trust Me when I speak. Take the difficult road I give you, and watch the Master work it out far beyond what you imagined. I will never give you more than you can handle. Your covering from Me will carry you. Don't compromise with the world. They never know what they're doing. They always profess to be wise and have all the answers, and they just become fools. There is a new and living way, walk you in it. Here, with Me, that's the adventure you're looking for.

April 28

Romans 12:2

And be not conformed to this world; but be ye transformed by the renewing of your mind, that ye may prove what is that good, and acceptable, and perfect, will of God. KJV

So, you ask Me, "How can I change my brain, my mind, so that I can think clearly on the things of Christ?" You ask Me this quite often, if you will take note. The renewing of your mind is a process. The transformation is incredible. As you are transformed it proves all that is good and acceptable and perfect in the will of God. Think outside the box for a moment. Take yourself out of you and look for a moment. Look at the mind. This is key to your walk with Christ. The mind is an incredible thing. It holds all the memories, the aspirations, the 'feelings', the intents, the issues of the heart, the past, the present, the future. This is Satan's number one target. Your mind. Guard it. Keep it pure. As you let the world in it is destroyed by sin bit by bit. Think of the depraved, they seem unnatural. Of course, they do to the moral person. Morals tend to keep the mind in some array of decency. But as the mind strays into depravity so goes the actions. For instance, if you fill your life with porn, your life goes to perversion. An absolute given. Total road of destruction. If the engineer fills his life with building plans, he goes to sleep thinking about them and how to make them better. When you fill your life with Christ, however, it is a much more intense and spiritual act. Hell custom makes arrows for the mind. The porn addict is an easy distraction. So easily bought off by any perversion, because of the addiction. He already feels condemned and lost. No convincing involved any more. The engineer has more 'noble' thoughts. His distractions are still there, but he can reason missing prayer or church because of overtime on this new project. He believes he has no need of Me, really. He thinks he has this under control. But then there's the committed Christian. The attacks are more structured and vicious. Hell has to sift and dig to find that which will distract and cause sin. So, the scattered thoughts that seem to come from nowhere and don't even seem tempting, nor even seem to be your own thoughts, because they aren't, those are fiery darts. Those are the things hell is blasting - trying to find a foothold. You must stay in My Word daily. Morning prayer is critical. Church services will change your life, one at a time, because of the preaching. As you fight each attack, hold your ground, the renewing is established. Like building a muscle. The more you work on that particular muscle, the stronger it becomes. I have to allow the attacks, to build you. But it is through Christ that you fight it. You have the same brain, mind, as the guy down the road fighting addictions. Your choices renew it. His do not. Your choices bring strength, his bring weakness and crippling. Be strong, but in Christ. Remember where the strength comes from. Cast sin out, bring all thoughts into captivity. I got this. This is your maturity and growth.

Jeremiah 51:17

Every man is brutish by his knowledge; every founder is confounded by the graven image: for his molten image is falsehood, and there is no breath in them. KJV

When man creates a statue, when man gives it eyes that cannot see, ears that cannot hear, then bows down and expects it to do something for him, my jealousy is fueled. Not only does that affect Me, it also affects the foolish man. The nonsense of it is in itself contemptible. The sicknesses it opens a door to is a whole other issue. Have you seen them, the idol worshippers? They are bent over in sickness and bitterness. Their faces, teeth, backs, feet, contort. Their end is worse than their beginning. Not only zero growth as a Christian on this earth, but a falling backwards into demise and ruin. As Satan fell from heaven he took with him 1/3 of My angels. They are no longer beautiful, they are hideous demons, frightening to behold. Deception is a powerful tool. As Adam and Eve followed in rebellion to another's voice and promptings - so is the fool who longs from a piece of wood or clay a voice and direction. I am your creator. None other. The created cannot create its own creator. The ridiculousness of this is beyond explanation. It is pure deception. When entire churches worship and burn candles and sing songs of praise to statues and idols, entire peoples are cursed. You absolutely cannot worship the idol, nor display it, nor wear its trinkets about your neck, without causing an open door for hell to rush in and allow havoc and destruction in your life. Be 'not' deceived. Follow Me. Trust Me. I am a jealous God and there is no other before Me.

Jeremiah 51:47 Therefore, behold, the days come, that I will do judgment upon the graven images ... KJV

Matthew 24:45-47

Who then is a faithful and wise servant, whom his lord hath made ruler over his household, to give them meat in due season? Blessed is that servant, whom his lord when he comes shall find so doing. Verily I say unto you, That he shall make him ruler over all his goods. KJV

When I give a task to one of Mine, I expect them to perform the task. I have given them all of the resources, power and wisdom to complete it. It is of course up to my servant to tap into the resources available, to seek Me when they feel weak or unable, and to seek My wisdom when they find themselves in confusion. These areas will need to be addressed with each task. The remedies are clear. You are in a training, a shaping, a molding, and of course the task is beyond you. That is the point. I expect failure. I need perseverance. A continual pressing on your part, that is where the growth comes, the wisdom imparted, and your destiny is built. You can do this, but always remember only through Me. To have fruit in My kingdom, you must perform the task at hand.

May 1

Psalms 4:4

Stand in awe, and sin not; commune with your own heart upon your bed, and be still. KJV

When you need the power to avoid sin, stop and think on this. Look at the power strip on your desk. Unless the cord is plugged into it, there will be no power running to the appliance. You are struggling and want to stop the habit of something, -- sin. Plug into Christ. There is the water when you are thirsty. Drink of Me. That's My Word. Read it. Add to it prayer and praise. Pray and praise out loud.

These few things will quench your thirst for the sin. It is what will overcome in the midst of temptation. Also, your testimony is critical. Tell somebody you are saved, and Jesus is your savior. If you follow these instructions you will find the peace you are looking for at the end of your day.

May 2

Luke 21:29-32

And he spoke to them a parable; Behold the fig tree, and all the trees; When they now shoot forth, ye see and know of your own selves that summer is now nigh at hand. So likewise ye, when ye see these things come to pass, know ye that the kingdom of God is nigh at hand. Verily I say unto you, This generation shall not pass away, till all be fulfilled. KJV

You know the seasons. Many times, I have reminded you, "Trust Me, this is but a season." Again, I remind you. Trust and carry on. When I say a season, I refer to a time when the page will turn and your struggle and trial will become a part of past memories. Learn from this season. Most often it will help the season pass more quickly by. Other times it will not and will try you in the fire; creating tremendous patience that will manifest in your life. That's Me when it does, that is a fruit of Me, My Spirit. When you see it manifest where it normally wasn't, that's how you'll know it's Me. I truly do carry you. More times than you realize. I love you so much, far beyond what you are able to comprehend at this moment. Life is hard. Heaven is worth it. I long for the day when you walk through those gates. Your joy will blow your mind. Be strong, in Me.

Jeremiah 51:15

He hath made the earth by his power, he hath established the world by his wisdom, and hath stretched out the Heaven by his understanding. KJV

You ask for power, you ask for wisdom, you ask for understanding. I create, establish and finish by these things. So, shall you. You create with the words you speak, you establish with the encouragement you say out loud, you finish with praise and worship. Think on this for a moment. The power, wisdom, and understanding of the Creator of heaven and earth, He gives you access to. Be very slow to speak. You do not have to say every thought that flips through your head. This is wisdom. Take care with the folks I place in your hands, you establish My kingdom in their lives with the encouragement you bring them. Always praise, worship and glorify and remember thanksgiving to the One who gave these things to you. This is the finishing of your faith. Stand tall. You're standing with Me.

Tired?

Matthew 24:42

Watch therefore; for ye know not what hour your Lord doth come. KJV

Weariness. I know you're weary. I know you're worn down. I know this because you are busy with the tasks I have given you. The Kingdom of God is built by tired people. These are the people I can trust to carry on, play "hurt"' and do what needs to be done; no matter the 'feelings' they endure. Well rested folks usually are that way because they are not working at what I have given them. My grace is sufficient for you though. I will carry you. However, in the midst of the labor at hand, you must keep your eyes on Me. I am coming as a thief in the night. The thief comes at night when the household is asleep, not expecting his appearance. When I said, "Do not weary of well doing," it was because it is what happens when saints forget I'm coming. Your face picks up, your pace picks up, your countenance and strength pick up, when you watch for Me. When you remember this is only for a season and rest is at hand, the load lightens. I am coming. You can be sure of that. Look for Me, count on Me, speak to Me, spend time with Me, that's the rest you seek, that's the watch I speak of. By the way, stay busy with My work, it's a lot lighter than the world's.

May 5

Psalms 122:1

I was glad when they said unto me, Let us go into the house of the Lord. KJV

People who live without a church will never experience this joy. The sheer joy of Sunday morning prep, getting prepared for a service with a community of believers who love and care for each other. It is your responsibility to find and gather with such a people. Do not tell Me you are too weary. Do not speak to Me of worn and torn. Leave the world behind for a while. Leave the flesh and all its desires fallen to the floor. Pick up, get ready, and enter My house with a joy. Smile at someone today that is struggling in their faith. Bring someone with you that is curious about Me. Tell someone they're beautiful and lovely. Speak softly, drench in My presence. Sing loudly, stand in My presence. Love soundly, enjoy and share My presence. Somebody needs you on a Sunday morning, a Sunday evening, a midweek service and bible study group. If not you, then who? This My friend, is living for God. Give of yourself. Even if you're weary. We have much work to do. You will rest in heaven. Here on earth? Well, get busy.

Jeremiah 50:24-25

.... Thou art found and also caught, because thou hast striven against the Lord. The Lord hath opened his armoury, and hath brought forth the weapons of his indignation.... KJV

.... That's what you get for taking on God. I, God, opened my arsenal, I brought out my weapons of wrath. ... The Message

When My people are assaulted, when My people are persecuted, I take this very personal. Do not count My taking strategic timing and strategy - as a failure to respond. I will respond. I will open My arsenal to respond to remove your enemy. Many times, when you seem to be waiting for an answer, the answer is on its way, within a hands grasp. Be patient with My timing. It is always right and always strategic. I am God. I am serious when it comes to defending Mine. I am also serious about molding and shaping you in these times of your trials. Respond correctly, with patience, perseverance, and trust. Do not moan. These actions on your part allow Me to move the way I want to. Work with Me. I got this, and so do you!

May 7

Deuteronomy 18:13

Thou shalt be perfect with the Lord thy God. KJV

I look for perfect. When I make a command, it is not an option. My authority has the right to command. My Word has authority, with commands that are to help you, not impede you. To be victorious you must follow My commands. You know you're far from perfect. When I said perfect, I meant, blameless, absolutely true to Me. This that I am calling you to is a privilege. That's why you need Jesus Christ. He doesn't see your sin. Jesus makes you blameless.

What is sin? It is missing the mark. It is knowing what is right and not doing it. I will hold you to account. This is a principle of life. If you want Me to do any good with your life, you better get this down. If you want to be acceptable, you must strive for perfection without a divided heart.

You are created to serve, specifically to achieve a purpose, a role, in life - for My will and purposes. Sin removes you from that. Most people don't have any idea that they have a purpose in Me. Selfishness of the human heart takes the sacrifice of Christ for granted. 'Just enough to get into heaven' attitude. This attitude will cause you to miss out on what I have for you. I want all of you. When you realize, and act upon that, living for Me will become easier. I search the heart, for the intent. It's great you're there, but why? Only I can give you that perfect heart. Pray and meet with Me. The perfect heart is a gift from Me to Mine. Align your life with Me, get involved with the building of the kingdom, seek it, contend for it, that's where I can soften and mold the heart.

May 8

Proverbs 15:1

A soft answer turneth away wrath; but grievous words stir up anger. KJV

Have you noticed yet that when you are kind to people it helps them to put down their sword of defense and you have a pleasant time with them? This is how I want you to conduct yourself in most instances and interchanges with people. Many times, conflicts arise, remember to treat people how you would like to be treated even in the midst of a conflict. Love and respect. Have a heart for them, it will go a long way when you have to shoulder the hurt sometimes and not retaliate as the flesh would love to do. A soft answer will help immensely. Guard your words, they don't have to be many. Well placed words from someone who cares and is not always correcting go a long long way with folks. Plant seed. Don't expect results immediately. Trust Me to help you with conversations. I will. I'm always with you. Just turn and see Me. I can guide you even with your tongue. It is easier to win someone who is not angry, although you will face persecution and anger over My Word. Just pay attention to Me. I'll help you sort through this thing called life and give you wisdom in your circumstances.

May 9

Titus 3:14

And let ours also learn to maintain good works for necessary uses, that they be not unfruitful. KJV

Our people have to learn to be diligent in their work so that all necessities are met (especially among the needy) and they don't end up with nothing to show for their lives.   The Message

Christians are called to many things. Not one Christian is able to perform every ministry that is needed in a body of believers. I call you to do your part. Your calling is a tremendous privilege. Remember to count it as such. When you moan and complain about it, difficulties arise in the saints that surround you. Bring your labors and sacrifices with a joy. And it would be great if you would smile and give the glory to Christ for the changing of your life. As you do your part, others in turn can perform theirs. Brick upon brick, watch how great that works. Trust Me with your life. You are not saved by works, however the work needs to be done, and I have called you to it. I have entrusted these tasks to you. Be diligent and faithful. I will bless your labors. I will bless you beyond what you are expecting. Heaven is coming. Carry on.

May 10

Exodus 20:12

Honor thy father and thy mother; that thy days may be long... KJV

This commandment comes with a promise of long life. There is absolutely no way I can bless your life if you do not keep and uphold this commandment. Your parents are human, and have many flaws. But then so do you. They are your authority in the earth from when you were formed. Forgive them for the wrongs. Your job is to honor them. I will take care of the judgments and the righting of the wrongs. Pray blessing on them and cease any talk of cursing upon them. Love them, and I will bless you with long life. I wrote this commandment in stone, so you would never forget I spoke it. I take it very very seriously.

May 11

Lamentations 3:55-57

I called upon thy name, O Lord, out of the low dungeon. Thou hast heard my voice: hide not thine ear at my breathing, at my cry. Thou drewest near in the day that I called upon thee: thou saidst, Fear not. KJV

Many days in life will come when the separation between heaven and earth will seem so vast and insurmountable. Be still and know that I am God. I am right here. Come to Me. Call upon My name and I will help. Keep a right heart and it allows me to move. Stubbornness stalls blessing. So does pride, hate, envy, these are the enemies of the heart. Study and look at yourself. Take time to step out of the box and look at your heart. Repent for what you see is amiss and encroaching on you. Then I am able to draw near. Fear not. I am able to help. I want to heal the heart and send your spirit soaring.

Lamentations 3:58 ....thou hast redeemed my life   KJV

The Ministry of Reconciliation

2 Corinthians 5:17-20

Therefore if any man be in Christ, he is a new creature; old things are passed away; behold, all things are become new. And all things are of God, who hath reconciled us to himself by Jesus Christ, and hath given to us the ministry of reconciliation, To wit, that God was in Christ, reconciling the world unto himself, not imputing their trespasses unto them; and hath committed unto us the word of reconciliation. Now then we are ambassadors for Christ ...
KJV

First yourself, then others around you. They become your number one job. Conversion produces evidence, the fruits of repentance, the new creature. Witness when you can, when they are open, when they are not open. Speak My Word to sinners. They won't hear it anywhere else. Be My voice crying in the wilderness - preaching repent. It is the foolishness of preaching that saves them. It is the most beautiful word the human can ever hear, repent. For it unlocks the door to salvation and eternal life.

May 13

Matthew 20:16

So the last shall be first, and the first last; for many be called, but few chosen. KJV

It's not how you start, it's how you finish. Take a look at yourself. Are your morals lining up with My Word? Or are they looking more like the world's? Repent, give your all to Me. I cannot work with half of a heart. I want it all. I want it today. I must be about the work of molding and finishing your faith. Trust My decisions. Give Me all of the trash in your life, right at the altar. How else can I cleanse you? Lest I take it all and wash it into the sea of forgetfulness. And would you take it a step farther this time? Don't come back picking through the trash trying to salvage those things of your old life. Just give it all to Me, the whole bag full, and look forward. I will fill your hands with a new life.

May 14

Genesis 11:31

..and they went forth from Ur to the land of Canaan; and they came unto Haran, and dwelt there.   KJV

This is a glimpse into Abraham. I called him to leave his kindred and his home and go to Canaan. My will for his life and destiny for his descendants was in Canaan. He stopped in Haran. He thought his idea was best. I had to remind him again. It is recorded a couple of verses later.

Genesis 12:1

..Get thee out...I will show you   KJV

My question to you is this: have you settled for Haran, when I have called you to Canaan? Do you honestly believe your way is better than mine? Somehow Abraham got stuck in Haran. He settled for less. He did not want to go all the way. He didn't want to strive for that new life any longer. He got comfortable. His father influenced him. Who is influencing your choices? I am calling you. I am reminding you again. Stop and pray today. I have a destiny and purpose for you. You will not fulfill it by sitting in that same spot. You need to get up and be about your Father's business. Take a look at Samson. He slowly gave himself to compromise. When he turned around and needed the power I had given him, it was no longer there. Where is your power today? Is it accessible? Or have you wandered so far off into compromise you didn't even realize you had gotten stuck in Haran?

May 15

Ezekiel 3:17-23

Son of man, I have made thee a watchman unto the house of Israel; therefore hear the word at my mouth and give them warning from me.

When I say to the wicked, Thou shalt surely die; and thou givest him not warning, nor speakest to warn the wicked from his wicked way, to save his life; the same wicked man shall die in his iniquity; but his blood will I require at thine hand.

Yet if thou warn the wicked, and he turn not from his wickedness, nor from his wicked way, he shall die in his iniquity; but thou hast delivered thy soul.

Again, When a righteous man doth turn from his righteousness, and commit iniquity, and I lay a stumblingblock before him, he shall die; because thou hast not given him warning, he shall die in his sin, and his righteousness which he hath done shall not be remembered; but his blood will I require at thine hand.

Nevertheless if thou warn the righteous man, that the righteous sin not, and he doth not sin, he shall surely live, because he is warned; also thou hast delivered thy soul.

And the hand of the Lord was there upon me; and he said unto me, Arise, go forth into the plain, and I will there talk with thee.

Then I arose, and went forth into the plain; and, behold, the glory of the Lord stood there, as the glory which I saw by the river of Chebar; and I fell on my face. KJV

When I speak, you need to listen. Ezekiel's prophecies and visions were recorded for you, not just for dusty shelves. Look up. I'm speaking to you. They sit around you every day, within arm's reach, and yet you claim to know Me, but refuse to share My saving grace with them. If you would but turn to them and tell them I have the answers and hope they are looking for, you would see revival break out. Just try those simple words and invite them to a church service and see what I will do in the midst of you and this generation. They are your responsibility. You are the watchman of your generation. I do not change, I am the same yesterday, today and forever.

May 16

John 11:8-10

His disciples say unto him, Master, the Jews of late sought to stone thee; and goest thou thither again?

Jesus answered, Are there not twelve hours in the day? If any man walk in the day, he stumbleth not, because he seeth the light of this world.

But if a man walk in the night, he stumbleth, because there is no light in him. KJV

When I direct your paths, and you trust My leading you, you walk in the light. When you attempt to accomplish things on your own, this is like stumbling around in the dead of night. Don't you find things easier if you take care of them in the light of the day. Aren't you even more refreshed in countenance. Consider the countenance of the one who insists on shift work. Working the midnight hours or the late hours and not taking to his home and locking his door when the darkness falls. It changes everything about him. Not only the spiritual countenance but the physical as well. So also with those that insist on doing things their own way. It may work in some respects. But they will never blossom and be who I have called them to be when they refuse to walk in the light of the day, nor the light of My Son. Come, let Me turn the light on for you. Start with morning prayer. End with the lights out while you rest. I will bring the rest, and in the morning, I will bring the light. Then you can walk into danger if need be, only because you walk in My light, and you see full well what you are called to and what you are walking into. Stay prayed up My saint. We have much work to do.

May 17

Psalms 119:64

Train me to live by your counsel. KJV

If you would do what I speak to you each day, you would find that my directions are your 'Training 101' series. I train you through My Word, headship, life experiences and interaction with others. The bumps, the bruises, along the way bring training you can receive no other way. Remember and think on the curious soul. The one who's head is up, paying attention to what is happening around them. Remember I am always at work. I am at work in and around you. Look for what I am doing and move in that direction. Play hurt, do not become paralyzed. People who won't and do become paralyzed are paralyzed by fear. Fear is a spirit. You must work against it. Fear attempts to keep you from recognizing My will for you today. In My training you will always find opposition. Fear is the number one card hell will pull on you today. Press in and press through. Look what I'm doing. Move with Me. No matter what.

Genesis 28:16-17

And Jacob awaked out of his sleep, and he said, Surely the Lord is in this place; and I knew it not.

And he was afraid, and said, How dreadful is this place! this is none other but the house of God, and this is the gate of heaven. KJV

Jacob built an altar that day. He made a reference point for himself and in so doing, also for every single person that should read My Word.

Reference points are critical in your walk with Me. Without them, the human mind forgets who I am, where I met you, and how I changed you. As you set road markers, reference points - I am able to give you a visual reminder of where you came from. Jacob found Me that day, and wasn't looking. Many days you seek Me and can't seem to see Me. That is sin and distrust that hide Me from you. Jacob's name was 'thief'. What is yours? What sin so taints your spiritual vision that you cannot find a Creator who is everywhere, including, residing inside of your heart since the day you accepted Christ as your Lord and Savior? What sin frustrates your walk with Me, dilutes your spiritual vision? When I seem far away, take time to do a heart check. I will help you with that.

John 11:16

That's when Thomas, the one called Twin, said to his companions, "Come along. We might as well die with him." The Message

Thomas was a doubter and looked on the dark side of life many times. In this scripture he was concerned for himself, not Me. He really didn't want Me to go to Lazarus because of the tension of the religious people against Me at the time. I was able to use him after the resurrection. However, he needed a physical appearance of my scars to believe I was resurrected. Do you? Will you trust Me today, even when I do not move in the way, the shape, the form, the speed, along the exact paths, you expect Me to? Faith believes, like Mary. Remember Lazarus's sister? She was always at My feet, waiting with expectancy and love. She trusted Me. Walk and learn of Me. I know you have much to do today. I know there is so much on your plate. Take time for Me. I will help with that. I want to be involved in your life. I am able.

May 20

Genesis 1:27-28

So God created man in his own image, in the image of God created he him; male and female created he them. And God blessed them, and God said unto them, Be fruitful, and multiply, and replenish the earth, and subdue it; and have dominion over the fish of the sea, and over the fowl of the air, and over every living thing that moveth upon the earth. KJV

Be fruitful, have that first born and love him with a huge heart. Raise him in the things of Me. When he is older he shall not depart. Show him Me, always. Show him My will, always. Teach him righteousness, always. Never ever ever compromise with right.

Discipline him so he understands righteousness. Discipline with a loving hand, not one of hate and indifference. Care for the child. Love and nurture, feed well, nourish and encourage the physical and the spiritual out of love and joy. Always let him know your love, so that he will understand Mine as well. When you fail, as you will sometimes, be ready to apologize and correct the issue. Then trust Me with him. I love Him more than you, more than you will ever understand. Then have more wonderful babies and your oldest will help in the molding of them as well. Smile and laugh, but be sober and vigilant. Life is short.

May 21

Psalms 11:7

For the righteous Lord loveth righteousness; his countenance doth behold the upright. KJV

I do not waiver from right and I love when you make a right decision. This is righteousness. The righteous will see Me. Are you a person of integrity? all the time? continually, consistently, always striving? Who are you trying to please? Will you give up your claims and rights to self? Are you willing to surrender your grasp on everything you call yours? Paul finally understood, he told you, to live is Christ, to die is gain. James understood a double minded person receives nothing from Me, because double mindedness is evidence of instability. Will you make heaven your home? If you cannot do these things, you will not. I must have all of you, not a piece of you. Look again and search your heart. If you cannot bear to look, ask Me, I will show you bit by bit and help you to be an overcomer.

Ezekiel 11:5

And the Spirit of the Lord fell upon me, and said unto me, Speak;
Thus saith the Lord; Thus have ye said, O house of Israel: for I
know the things that come into your mind, every one of them. KJV

I am God. I am your Creator. I know you inside and out. I have
molded and shaped you to be a peculiar person. You are made
different than any other soul I have placed on earth since the
beginning of time. Your purpose is different than any other I have
made. I have set you apart, called you to a specific time, a time such
as this. Meet with Me. I have much to reveal and show to you. I can
only do this when we meet together. Read My Word. Ponder on each
mystery I reveal to you. Put it in your mind. Put it into action. Many
read and read - and their tattered worn bibles show it, their scholarly
countenance displays they comprehend it, however, their double
mindedness reveals their lack of putting it into action. Run with Me.
Don't look back. This truly is a wild adventure. But it is an adventure
worth living. This is life. This is YOUR great adventure. I will never
leave you, nor forsake you. Even until the end of the world.

May 23

1 Thessalonians 4:15

For this we say unto you by the word of the Lord, that we which
are alive and remain unto the coming of the Lord shall not prevent
them which are asleep. For the Lord Himself shall descend from
heaven with a shout, with the voice of the archangel, and with the
trump of God; and the dead in Christ shall rise first. Then we
which are alive and remain shall be caught up together with them

in the clouds, to meet the Lord in the air; and so shall we ever be with the Lord. KJV

I ask you to encourage each other with these words. Comfort each other. Why? This my dear is the blessed hope. I told you I was coming back, simply because I am. I'm coming back for a peculiar people, the ones who are working, the ones who I have chosen and have responded, the ones that have been set aside. Be not deceived in these last days. I am always always responding to your needs and prayers. Wait. Your blessing is within a hand's grasp, almost right in your hand. Stand firm, stand strong, even when you just don't feel like it. Draw close to Me, let Me cover you. When you are washed over with feelings of condemnation from apparent past failures, look up, repent, trust Me, they have all been washed away. Dry your eyes. Let's do this. Carry on with what I have called you to today. I still have that plan! I still have your back. Hell loves to use past failures to draw you down and into unbelief. That's a diversion, and many times a successful one. Do not let it be so in your life. Look up, straighten your back, and move forward. The devil is a liar and the father of all lies. Walk with Me in deliverance and strength and truth. Look to the right, look to the left, there is much work to be done. You are Mine.

May 24

Galatians 4:31

So then, brethren, we are not children of the bond woman, but of the free. KJV

You are born of the Spirit. You are born of the promise. You are not held captive of the flesh. The flesh was done away with at the cross. You are My child by faith in Christ Jesus. You are justified by that faith. No longer will you say, I hope I am saved, I hope I make heaven, but by faith you will speak, I am justified by my faith in Christ, I am a child of God. When you speak these words, without hesitation, the Spirit I have placed in your heart, the Spirit of My Son, will leap, and display the evidence. Walk in faith. I will rock your world.

May 25

Exodus 20:12

Honour thy father and thy mother; that thy days may be long upon the land which the Lord thy God giveth thee. KJV

This is the only one of the 10 I gave Moses inscribed on the tablets that had a promise attached. There is a natural peace and blessing in a person's life that honors their parents. The rebellious one quite often is the one that was not disciplined properly as a child. It is critical a child learns how to process right and wrong, disappointments and setbacks, victories and accomplishments, and to learn that the parent and others are authorities in their lives, but especially the parent. The child finds no peace without learning these things, from as small as an infant who can't sleep if mother's arms aren't always around them to a 3-year-old who can't walk through an aisle of a grocery store without being able to take with him everything he demands. The teen age years are difficult enough as they begin to see the things of the world tempting and alluring them away from the home structure and disciplines, if added to that is a home where authority never won its place in the teen's character, it will be insurmountable for them to survive with their integrity still intact. I set your parents as an example of My authority in your life. This is the structure I expected mankind to operate in. Honor Me by honoring them. I knew there would be flaws, things you wouldn't understand, honor them for Me. Look right past them when you are frustrated and finding it difficult- and see Me.

May 26

Ephesians 6:10-12

Finally, my brethren, be strong in the Lord, and in the power of his might.

Put on the whole armour of God, that ye may be able to stand against the wiles of the devil.

For we wrestle not against flesh and blood, but against principalities, against powers, against the rulers of the darkness of this world, against spiritual wickedness in high places. KJV

Never ever forget your armor. It is critical in your walk with Me. You wrestle master spirits. Their goal is to destroy you. Do not carry on today as if there is no battle raging around you. No soldier in his right mind would ever enter a battlefield without the armor.

Ephesians 6:13-18

Wherefore take unto you the whole armour of God, that ye may be able to withstand in the evil day, and having done all, to stand.

Stand therefore, having your loins girt about with truth, and having on the breastplate of righteousness;

And your feet shod with the preparation of the gospel of peace;

Above all, taking the shield of faith, where with ye shall be able to quench all the fiery darts of the wicked.

And take the helmet of salvation, and the sword of the Spirit, which is the Word of God:

Praying always with all prayer and supplication in the Spirit ...for all saints. KJV

Proverbs 27:5

A spoken reprimand is better than approval that's never expressed.
The Message

Open rebuke is better than secret love. KJV

How will you learn unless you are told? How will they learn unless
they are taught? If you tell them and they do not follow, use another
method. Take dominion. Teach. Find the art of ministry. The art of
ministry is getting people to do what they wouldn't normally do. Not
manipulation. That's crossing the line. That is the spirit of witchcraft.
Ministry allows them to be changed by exampleship of course and
more importantly by Me. Pray for them. But teach them. I've put you
in a position with them that no one else on the earth has. Influence
for Christ. You can do it. Ask Me. I want to help you with that.

Psalm 24:1

The earth is the Lord's, and the fullness thereof; the world, and
they that dwell therein. KJV

I did create the world. This makes it Mine. I did create everything in
it. This makes all of it Mine. I did create you. This makes you Mine.

Psalms 24:4-10

He that hath clean hands, and a pure heart; who hath not lifted up
his soul unto vanity, nor sworn deceitfully. He shall receive the
blessing from the Lord, and righteousness from the God of his
salvation.

Who is this King of glory? The Lord strong and mighty.

Who is this King of glory? The Lord of hosts, he is the King of glory. KJV

You belong to the King. You belong to Me. Clean hands and a pure heart keep you close to Me. This also opens the door to My blessing. My righteousness and salvation will cover and keep you. Stay--- close! You truly are Mine.

May 29

Ezekiel 18:30-32

Therefore I will judge you, O house of Israel, everyone according to his ways, saith the Lord God. Repent, and turn yourselves from all your transgressions; so iniquity shall not be your ruin.

Cast away from you all your transgressions, whereby you have transgressed; and make you a new spirit: for why will you die, O house of Israel?

For I have no pleasure in the death of him that dieth, saith the Lord God: wherefore turn yourselves and live ye. KJV

When you continually sin, and refuse to repent I have no choice but to bring judgment. The blood of My Son was shed for you so that you might turn from sin and have access to all of My power and strength to defeat sin's hold on you. Look at the drug addicted. They will sell their own children for another hit. So is sin in a human's life. The grip is so strong, there is nothing the human will not do to hold tight. The only difference between the drug addicted and most sinners is the evidence of the stronghold to others. Do not believe for a moment that you have any victories without My Spirit. The devil would deceive you, as he did Adam, as he did Eve. I am for you, not against you. My pleasure is in your victories, definitely not in your defeats. Failures do serve a purpose in My kingdom: teach, mold and shape. Why? Because all things work together for good for those that love Me and are called to My purpose. Unrepented hearts are evidence of a heart very far from Me. Repented hearts show love towards Me and make Me burst with joy. Come to Me, with those heavy burdens. Let Me give you that rest. Lay it all down for goodness sakes.

May 30

1 Peter 5:7

Casting all your care upon him; for he careth for you. **KJV**

Live carefree before God; he is most careful with you.
The Message

Peter got this. He understood, after so many mistakes and challenges along his way, that I took great care for him, I was careful with him. His destiny was far beyond this world and he knew it. He laid it all on the line in a martyr's death, but also in a disciple's life. As I molded and shaped him, he began to realize the thought and care and plans I had for him. Never has one man laid so much aside as this one. The material things of course, but I am talking about the prejudices, the attitudes, the hardness of heart. All of these bubbled to the surface in full view for all mankind throughout history to use as reference points even in their own lives. He kept few things hidden that were initially between himself and Me. He aired his flaws in arrogance many times, but also as a testimony of a changed life, he willingly allowed himself to be in the spotlight of the kingdom in humility. This brought Me glory, also, it brought him life and life more abundantly. When you make mistakes, errors, be humble and accept correction. It will change your destiny, and bring Me glory.

Colossians 1:17

And he is before all things, and by him all things consist. KJV

Colossians 1:19

For it pleased the Father that in him should all fullness dwell; KJV

Colossians 2:6

As ye have therefore received Christ Jesus the Lord, so walk ye in him: KJV

Colossians 2:9

For in him dwellest the fullness of the Godhead bodily. KJV

Colossians 2:10

And ye are complete in him .. KJV

Colossians 3:9,10,11

..put off the old man .. put on the new man .. Christ is all in all .. KJV

Folks who walk in Christ walk in the fullness of God the Father. Your brain can not comprehend all that that gives you access to. Trust in Me when I say, lift up your head, walk in My ways, and demons will tremble and flee, sin will no longer have dominion in your life, addictions will fall away. You are a warrior, and more, a victorious one, only because you walk in My fullness. The victory won on Calvary's cross cannot all be understood by the mind you have now, but it can be experienced. Leave the old man behind, you are brand new in Christ. Shame and guilt are washed away. Mind battles are no more, when you allow Me to fight them instead of you. Love and life replace all of that. Joy and victory is your countenance. It's a brand new wild ride, enjoy it!

JUNE

June 1

Galatians 6:8-9

..he that soweth to the Spirit shall of the Spirit reap life everlasting.
And let us not be weary in well doing; for in due season we shall
reap, if we faint not. KJV

Much of your weariness comes from lack of strategy. You are
forgetting to strategize. Does a builder build without a plan? Never.
Does a God who loves you orchestrate your life without a plan?
Never! I know the plans I have for you. It would do you well to
commune with Me and ask for help in strategizing your day of
course, but also the months ahead. There are people who would have

been lost lest you were there, right where I placed you, right in the condition I placed you, to be a landing field for them. Ask Me, I will show you. I never show you all, but I will show you how to strategize if you take time to ask.

June 2

Exodus 33:20

And he said, Thou canst not see my face; for there shall no man see me, and live. KJV

And so it is today, after the death and resurrection of My Son, Jesus Christ, you also with him are dead, yet shall you live. The closer you come to Me, and My holiness, the more the flesh dies, however, the more the 'new man' - which is you in Christ - the more the new man lives, comes alive and is dominant in your life. Moses didn't have access to the new man. He was before the resurrected Christ. Learn this. Sin kills, destroys and mutates. My presence shrivels all of that up as sin is forgiven and overcome. The new man comes alive and you stand tall in Christ as a warrior in the Kingdom. Your countenance in trials and fears may even reflect the shriveling, for a moment, as you make stands for Me, but your very countenance will dramatically shift as lessons are learned and battles are won. It's a spiritual thing, that reflects and gives evidence in the physical. Pay attention in your next trial. Watch Me move as you obey. This is the good stuff. This is the glory stuff. Hang in there. This is the exciting stuff. Look for Me. I'm right there with you.

John 11:5

Now Jesus loved Martha ... KJV

Luke 10:41-42

And Jesus answered and said unto her, Martha, Martha, thou art careful and troubled about many things; But one thing is needful; and Mary hath chosen that good part, which shall not be taken away from her. KJV

I always always always correct the ones I love. I was able to correct Martha because she loved Me. I was able to impart into her life because of the relationship we had together, even on this earth. She trusted Me to correct her, and I always followed through. I wanted her to be the best she could be. Sometimes she forgot that meant sitting down and just listening to Me. You don't always have to be cleaning and serving and doing. Sometimes it is just sitting in My presence and learning of Me. That is why I created you. For fellowship. It changes you, were you aware of that? Every single time you draw near to Me, you are changed, and that can definitely not be taken away from you. Come, sit with Me, listen for a while.

June 4

God's Champions

1 Samuel 22:1-2

David..escaped to the cave..they went down to him..

And every one that was in distress, .. in debt, ... was discontented, gathered themselves unto him; and he became a captain over them, .. four hundred men. KJV

HE KNOWS MY NAME

2 Samuel 23:8-39 (40 years later)

These be the names of the mighty men whom David had; ...

Adino ... He lift up his spear against eight hundred, whom he slew at one time..

Eleazar.. Arose and smote the Philistines until his hand was weary, and his hand clave unto the sword; and the Lord wrought a great victory ..

Shammah... He stood in the midst of the ground and defended it, and slew the Philistines; and the Lord wrought a great victory ..

Abishai .. Lifted up his spear against three hundred, and slew them ..

Benaiah.. Slew two lionlike men.... slew a lion in the midst of a pit in time of snow ... slew an Egyptian..a spear in his hand; but he went down to him with a staff, and plucked the spear out of the Egyptian's hand, and slew him with his own spear.   KJV

I record these men's names because of the honor they brought me in great battles. No man can do what they did on their own. I took those that were in distress, in debt and discontented for a reason. These were the ones I sent to David. He took time and worked with each of the four hundred, because I asked Him to. I built an earthly kingdom with them, but more importantly, I built a spiritual kingdom as well. So, as you look to this story as a reference point of Me choosing the outcasts and downtrodden of this world to confound the world, remember this, so were you. You were not the prize possession of the earth. But you are Mine. I treasure you beyond all things, because I see your potential, if you will give your all, step out in faith, step out in the impossible and do what I ask you to do. I will shape, mold, and make you into a valiant warrior for Christ. I will wrought greater victories than these through your life dedicated to

Me. Listen, I have direction for you. Obey, I have great adventures for you to experience. Run with me, your name will be written in the book of books, the Lamb's book of life.

June 5

Isaiah 61:10

I will greatly rejoice in the Lord, my soul shall be joyful in my God, for he hath clothed me with the garments of salvation, he hath covered me with the robe of righteousness, as a bridegroom decketh himself with ornaments, and as a bride adorneth herself with her jewels.   KJV

Find your joy in Me, my child. Find your joy in Me. There are issues in this world that will drag you around and make you feel unworthy. I am building you. Let Me mold you and shape you. Flaws are revealed as I am working on you. This causes your reactions of despair and hopelessness sometimes. Only because you are looking at the circumstances, the failures, all that I am trying to knead out of you, instead of the end purpose, your finishing and completion. Look up. I am right here. I am trying to fix it. Let go. Let Me.

June 6

Colossians 1:13-14

Who hath delivered us from the power of darkness, and hath transformed us into the kingdom of his dear Son;

In whom we have redemption through his blood, even the forgiveness of sin;   KJV

When you surrendered your life to Me, I delivered you from the power of darkness. I did that for a reason. I cannot have sin in My presence. I created you for fellowship with Me. How would I fellowship with someone who could not be in My presence? Only through the blood of Christ could your sin be washed away. As you repented, and surrendered your life to Me, all of that is washed clean. That is redemption. As you have been redeemed - so is redeemed - your place in My kingdom. I rescued you so that you no longer were bound by hell. Let loose of all that bound you. Shake it off. That is sanctification. You are sanctified by the renewing of the mind. Shake it off. You are sanctified by the reading of the Word. Shake it all off. You are sanctified by the Spirit of God. No longer addicted, set it aside, look towards Me. No longer a thief, let go. No longer a gossip, stop it. No longer a lover of evil, grab hold of the purpose I have for you. Pray in the mornings. Not a laundry list of things for Me to do for you, but a communion, a meeting with Me. Let Me be the Lord of your life. I will direct your paths, I will make them straight. Come along, I have a wonderful, exciting destiny - designed just for you - let's get to it!

June 7

Isaiah 61:1-3

The Spirit of the Lord is upon me; because the Lord hath anointed me ...

To appoint unto them that mourn in Zion, the oil of joy for mourning, the garment of praise for the spirit of heaviness; that they might be called trees of righteousness, the planting of the Lord, that he might be glorified.   KJV

When I gave you, this promise it was for more than what you were going through at the moment. I gave you this promise for all of your walk on this earth. You will be afflicted, you will come up short, you won't always win, there will always be trials and challenges, you are not on the easy road skipping through life without a care in the world. In fact, the more you press in, the more you serve, the more you have victories in the kingdom, the more you commune with Me, the more you make stands for Me, the more you are strengthened in the things of Me; the more hell marks you and strikes back. Think it not strange when you go through diverse temptations. Think it not odd when it seems the whole world is opposing you. Think it not unusual when there seems a battle on every front. Get your armor on. Then stand. Do everything you can to stand. And then stand. Watch what I do!

June 8

1 Corinthians 9:27

But I keep under my body, and bring it into subjection; lest that by any means, when I have preached to others, I myself should be a castaway. KJV

Isaiah 40:25-26

To whom then will ye liken me, or shall I be equal? saith the Holy One.

Lift up your eyes on high, and behold who hath created these things, that bringeth out their host by number; he calleth them all by names by the greatness of his might, for that he is strong in power; not one faileth. KJV

Pray and meditate on the holiness of God. I am your creator, your deliverer, your salvation. I hold the power to save, the power to heal, the power to set the stars in the heavens in multitudes - yet still know each of their names. Your discipleship is indeed an obstacle course. However, I have already defeated death, hell, and the grave for you. As you draw close to Me, I reveal Myself to you. Be ye holy, as I am holy. Paul understood this as the key to his victory. Paul feared me because I am the judge. Paul loved Me because I was his savior.

Jesus spoke more of the fears of hell than the glories of heaven. Look about you. This generation has lost its fear of God. Have you?

June 9

1 Kings 19:11-12

And he said, Go forth, and stand upon the mount before the Lord. And, behold, the Lord passed by, and a great and strong wind rent the mountains, and brake in pieces the rocks before the Lord; but the Lord was not in the wind; and after the wind an earthquake; but the Lord was not in the earthquake;

And after the earthquake a fire; but the Lord was not in the fire; and after the fire a still small voice.   KJV

Many times, I ask you to meet with Me. Mornings are My delight, and you know this. However, you must wait on Me. Have you ever had a 'conversation' with someone and they won't let you get a word in edgewise? How does that make you feel? Think on what I deal with when you bring a 'to do' list of tasks you want Me to do for you, every single time we meet? Somewhere you have forgotten - I am God - you are not. I know your needs, I expect you to voice them, however, you must take time to listen when I speak, and pay attention to My Spirit. I am not in every wind and conflict of the world. Many times, those are distractions to keep you from waiting on My voice. I have specific purpose for you today. Take time to listen. I'm pretty good at getting My point across, at voicing My directions, but it takes a listening ear, a willing heart, to know My voice. Look up, I'm right here! My grace is sufficient.

John 8:47

He that is of God heareth God's words; ye therefore hear them not, because ye are not of God.   KJV

Whose child, are you? Did the man down the street raise and instruct you? Or did what your father say over ride anything the neighbor said? If your father had the authority in your life, you listened to him. So also, if you claim I have authority in your life, you will listen to Me. And when you listened to your father, you reacted when he said, "Do this." If you did not, consequences followed. When I speak, it is reasonable to expect you to react with actions. Why would you call Me your Father, and not do what I ask you to do? Obedience is evidence of being Mine. If you do not do what I ask, you are definitely not Mine. If you cannot distinguish My voice, it is time to fast and pray and take time to listen to Me. Settle this once and for all. Whose child, are you?

Free Indeed

John 8:36

So if the Son makes you free, then you are unquestionably free. AMP

What is true in the physical is also true in the spiritual. Many wars were fought for freedom. But today the enemy is back. They tax, they oppress, they place in bondage. So, people must fight again to win freedom again. So also, you. Your freedom must be maintained. Many times, you wonder. "Haven't I been liberated?" Governments bring back taxes in another area, when they were already abolished over here. Those will never go away. But when you were made free from sin, it was final. Like this world's governments that need a people to tax to exist, so also the prince of this world, needs a people to oppress. He looks for a foothold, a legitimate right into your life. But My scripture, and My Son's death and resurrection, were the final statements. You are unquestionably free, clean. As the devil looks for a chink in your armor, look at Jesus. When He was tempted for a time in the desert, He fought back with the Word. The devil has a set pattern, a plan to draw you back into your old lifestyle, even your mind comes under assault, to entangle you in things until there's no way out. This is a real enemy, a real war. There is a spiritual demonic battle when you pray. You've been given your weaponry. Jesus used the Word. That Word is yours to use, it is the most powerful weapon ever given. It conquers nations, and saves cities. It is quick and powerful and alters destinies. You know the truth. Bring every argument back to the Word. Let them argue with Me, rather than you. Jesus said, "It is written". It's not open to debate any longer. It will change the whole theme of the battle. Jesus destroyed Satan with the Word. Jesus had no doubt, and spoke it as fact and with authority. How you speak and act is critical in your battle. You must know the Word, read it every day. You must speak the Word, change your vocabulary. You must believe the Word. You must walk in faith. Then you will have victory. Prayer is critical. Real faith will manifest in your life with your actions. Freedom can only be maintained as we fight for it with the two-edged sword.

June 12

Galatians 4:31

So then, brethren, we are not children of the bond woman, but of the free. KJV

Paul makes his case in this chapter of the reason you are no longer under the law. My Son, Jesus Christ, gave His life to make this happen. You are free. Free from sin of course, that was the purpose. Free to be in fellowship with Me, that's why I created you. Free from condemnation, the devil lies to you daily, dredging up the filth from the sea of forgetfulness, where I placed it. Free to be Mine. No longer a slave to the lies of hell. Shake it off. No longer bound by the addictions of this world. Shake them off. No longer a gossip. Love people just as they are. No longer filled with venom of hate. Do something nice for someone today. Your character is altered because I altered it. You do hear my voice. Because I speak. You do operate in the gifts, because I have given them to you. Pick up your head, set your eyes forward, you have a battle to fight today. No longer act, nor re-act as if you do not. Stand for right and be victorious. It is your reasonable service.

June 13

Psalm 51:7

Purge me with hyssop, and I shall be whiter than snow. KJV

Hyssop is actually from a mint family. In the Old Testament days, people did not have access to cleaners such as you do. They would use hyssop as a cleaning agent. Also, I instructed them to use it in ceremonial cleaning in the case of leprosy in Leviticus 14. In Exodus 12, I commanded the Israelites to use it to paint the door posts with lamb's blood in order for the angel of death to pass over their homes. In John 19, John recorded for Me, that the soldier offered My Son vinegar in a sponge, held on a hyssop. This was Christ's last act upon earth before the resurrection. When David asked Me to cleanse him with hyssop he understood the implication of the purification of hyssop. David understood that his sins haunted him. He carried them with him and was being tormented by them. He wanted them gone.

Your memories are a part of you. Actions have tremendous consequences in your life. They make you and develop you. Of course, it is best not to sin, however, all have sinned and fall short. As far as I am concerned, when I forgive, these sins are placed into a sea of forgetfulness. Gone and washed with the blood, the hyssop treatment of purification is a picture of it. When your memory brings it back, you must pray, seek, and read My Word. You have forgiveness, you have cleansing, but it is part of the battle until you come home. Mind battles will be there, put under the blood of Christ, they can be overcome. Do not allow hell to torment you. Give them to Me. It's part of maturity as a Christian. Look past other's faults and failures and see Me, and look past your own and see Me as well. You can do it through Me. Without Me, no. With Me, yes! Envision the hyssop. Meditate on it. This will help you. I used it for a reason, for them, for you. Living under My grace is an amazing adventure. Seize it and your will have victory. Run with it and you will have grace on others.

June 14

Psalm 52:8

But I am like a green olive tree in the house of God; I trust in the mercy of God for ever and ever.   KJV

My mercies are what will carry you through your struggles and trials on earth as you grow. Planted in My house, as a green olive tree, your growth is anointed with the oil of My Holy Spirit. The olive oil is a symbol of My Spirit. My oil will illuminate you, so that you may illuminate others. My oil will make your light shine like no other. My oil is good for your body, but so much more so the soul. Olive oil was used in the cleansing ceremonies of lepers along with the hyssop. A symbol of the sin washed away and one purified. The olive must be pressed and shaken to extract the oil. So, think it not strange when you must be shaken and pressed, to be conformed and brought to repentance. After the shaking the olive must be beaten and bruised to extract the first fruits, the best oil. As this world shakes and bruises and beats on you, humbleness will be your good fruit. You will never ever know humbleness without the trials of this life. This is why I tell you, rejoice in trials, find joy in the struggles, it is a mark of growth. Be patient in all things. If you are mine, you understand the pressed down and shaken together. My grace truly truly truly is sufficient. My oil will make you shine and bring My house glory.

June 15

Ephesians 6:16

Above all, taking the shield of faith, wherewith ye shall be able to quench all the fiery darts of the wicked. KJV

Be not deceived, I tell you this many times. The devil seeks who he may devour. Keep your faith up. That shield is indestructible. A warrior in battle without a shield is a dead warrior. A Christian in battle without a shield is a backslider. You will not make heaven, nor a single victory, without your shield of faith. Notice Paul notes this, "above all". Without faith it is absolutely impossible to please Me. Not one step towards heaven can you take without it. Double talk, maybes, I'm not sure, what ifs, they all lead to destruction. Get your confidence on, trust Me. Remember, it's Me. I am the creator of all things, nothing is too hard for Me. Change your vocabulary and your countenance will change with it. It's time for that growth in you. No longer, "I think I can", but "through Christ, I got this, I can do it." Step it up.

Romans 8:38-39

For I am persuaded, that neither death, nor life, nor Angels, nor principalities, nor powers, nor things present, nor things to come,

Nor height, nor depth, nor any other creature, shall be able to separate us from the love of God, which is in Christ Jesus our Lord. KJV

My love for you surpasses all of your understanding. Your human mind cannot grasp it. I am your Creator, your mentor, your strength, your life. Not only Savior, but your all in all. You are My bride. Come away with Me all the days of your life. Meet with Me in your mornings, and stay your mind on Me in your days. I'll cover and keep you as you rest in the evenings. Heaven waits breathlessly for your arrival one day. While on earth continue to be about your Father's business. It's all going to be alright. Trust Me.

Zechariah 2:8-10

For thus saith the Lord of hosts; After the glory hath he sent me unto the nations which spoiled you; for he that toucheth you toucheth the apple of his eye.

For, behold, I will shake mine hand upon them ..

Sing and rejoice, O daughter of Zion; for, lo, I come, and I will dwell in the midst of thee, saith the Lord. KJV

When I speak of you as 'the apple of my eye' that refers to the way I cherish you. I have a favor and grace on you that the rest of the world will never enjoy. When I threaten those who touch you, don't think I use those words in vain. I choose My words carefully. There is power in the words I speak. They create and they tear down. So, when I showed you and spoke to you to look around and see the plentiful fruit that I have used you to reach, that was for a purpose. When hell tries to speak in your ear, 'you have no fruit, no purpose in God's plan', you will just ponder these things I have shown you, time and again, and have them for a reference point. For you are the apple of My eye. Do you not strive to do right? Yes, you do. Do you not strive to learn and hear My voice? Yes, you do. Would I not use such a one in this earth in a powerful way? Yes, I will. Continue to meet with Me in the mornings. I have rest for you. I have the strength you seek. I will give you the wisdom you need. When you feel that stretch, know it's Me, bringing you growth, through grace and favor. Look not to the right or the left. Fear not the naysayers nor the enemy. Give no heed to their voices. Trust Me. Run with Me. We got this. It's called destiny. Carry on!

June 18

Zechariah 4:6-10

This is the word of the Lord unto Zerubbabel, saying, Not by might, nor by power, but by my spirit, saith the Lord of hosts.

Who art thou O great mountain? ..

For who hath despised the day of small things? KJV

I'm talking to Mine here, not the world. Who despises small beginnings? Do you? Never discount the small things. Never discount your work I have called you to as insignificant. I have called you to it. I have placed you here, on purpose, for a purpose. Look about you. Do you see what I have done? Do you see them come, looking for answers? There is no coincidence in where I have placed you. I need you where you are to work with those in your corner of the earth. Long to grow, but long for My will. The grass is not always greener over there. Life is not always easier over there. All is not a bed of roses over there. I have placed you where you are, be content in the work I have called you to. That is maturity, that is strength. Draw close to Me when you feel dissatisfied, I will help you with that. Look to Me, not the world, I am the way, the truth and the life. Follow Me.

June 19

Ephesians 4:2

With all lowliness and meekness, with longsuffering, forbearing one another in love   KJV

People need love. It is how I created them. It is the center of the core, the place where they receive their self-confidence and self-esteem. I am love, are you? Take time to love the unlovable today. When you see distress displayed on someone - take time for a kind word. They don't always need to be put in their place, although there are times for that. Sometimes they just need a kind word. Heap coals of fire, or conviction from Me, by just a kind act. It helps them more than you will know or understand. Practice kind words, it will all come back around. Some day you will need someone to have grace on you with a word in due season. Honor Me, be completely like Me.

June 20

Psalm 102:17-19

He will regard the prayer of the destitute, and not despise their prayer.

This shall be written for the generation to come: and the people which shall be created shall praise the Lord.

For he hath looked down from the height of his sanctuary; from heaven did the Lord behold the earth   KJV

Yes, I still look upon the earth and seek to meet your needs. Cry unto Me, I will give you rest. The life in your world is a challenge, however, with Me, your God, all things are possible. Do not discount the down trodden and the weak. If they will seek My face I will deliver them from addictions and sickness. Share My Word with them as well. Be no respecter of persons. The exact same resurrection power that changed you will change them, if they will repent and turn from their wicked ways and serve Me. I have not called you to decide who will hear My Word, but I have called you to speak My Word, in season, out of season, and to speak it to all the world. Each person is created with a free will. It is their choice to answer My call. Put your boldness on, there is a lost and dying generation tired of the destruction they live in.

June 21

Psalm 104

Bless the Lord, O my soul, O Lord my God, thou art very great; thou art clothed with honour and majesty. Who coverest thyself with light as with a garment; who stretchest out the heavens like a curtain   KJV

Take time today to sit in My presence. Think on the heavens. I created them for you. Think on the light that awaits you. There is a light in this world. It is Christ, My Son. He lights your way, He lights your heart, He lights your very countenance. Have you ever looked at a new convert, how their countenance changes immediately? So, you, have that light. Consider these things and draw close to Me today. I want to lighten your burden, this is where it begins.

Romans 5:8

But God commended his love toward us, in that, while we were yet sinners, Christ died for us. KJV

I did not wait for you to get cleaned up before I gave My Son for you. In your vilest, nastiest, meanest state, I saw you, and still the blood was shed to redeem you. You are Mine. Your reasonable service is to share My gospel with someone else today. Take time to look closely at the people I have placed in your life, almost as it seems, out of nowhere. They are the ones I want you to reach. While Jesus rested at the well, I brought folks to Him. I still do that today, while you are resting, or in obscure places, I will bring them to you. I ask you to reach them for Me. I died for them in their rough state. Love changes people. Well it changed you.

Acts 1:8

But ye shall receive power, after that the Holy Ghost is come upon you; and ye shall be witnesses unto me, both in Jerusalem, and in all Judaea, and in Samaria, and unto the uttermost part of the earth. KJV

People with power are people with the Holy Ghost indwelling in them. Do not be deceived, the power they claim over you is nothing they can have without My permission. Many times, I use them to affect your life, however, never be deceived into thinking they can do anything to you without My protection. Lift up your eyes and see Me in the circumstances. You have the dominion here, not them. You have the power here, not them. You have it good. They have it bad, even horrible. They take it out on you, but just take time to remember that I am here, I am your covering. Do not cower to fear and intimidation of bullies. Walk in Me. I got this.

June 24

Galatians 1:24

And they glorified God in me. KJV

When people meet you, hear you speak, watch how you behave, do they see Me? Am I glorified? Or is the world? Guard your testimony before men. I must be able to use you to make impact. When I expose flaws in your life, repent, ask Me to help you overcome. Grow, change, live the life of the renewed and changed man. You will never be the same, nor will you ever desire to be.

June 25

1 Thessalonians 3:12-13

And the Lord make you to increase and abound in love one toward another, and toward all men, even as we do toward you:

To the end he may stablish your hearts unblameable in holiness before God, even our Father, at the coming of our Lord Jesus Christ with all his saints. KJV

Pray for these things. Hell's number one goal is to frustrate and isolate the saint. You must love people. You must give and take time for them. Without this - your heart will never be established in holiness. Be ye holy, just because I am. I expect you to honor Me by becoming more like Me. When you run into difficulties doing that, stop and pray. You can love people. But it takes a willing heart towards Me. Look past them and see Me. I will help you.

Psalms 106:13

**They soon forget his works; they waited not for his counsel.
KJV**

Isn't it hard to go forward when you have no idea where you are
going? Take time for prayer this morning. Be specific, so that I in
turn have the opportunity to be specific with you. I want to guide and
direct you, however you so often run in your own direction -
sometimes it's harder for you to realize you need to get back on
track. Do not forget Me, nor neglect waiting on My counsel. This is
critical in your walk with Me. Ask and you will receive, I promise.

1 Thessalonians 3:2

*And sent Timotheus, our brother, and minister of God, and our
fellowlabourer in the gospel of Christ, to establish you, and to
comfort you concerning your faith: KJV*

Many times, you have needed to hear from Me. Church attendance is
critical in your walk with Me. Paying attention is also more
important. You take notes, and then neglect to make them a part of
your days. I give that message from your pastor to help you to grow.
Yes, it's great you're there to hear it. When you take those notes, it
solidifies it somewhat more in the natural brain, and so in the Spirit.
If you would take those notes out and refresh yourself in what I
spoke through your pastor, to you, you will find a treasure trove of
encouragement and strength. Do not discount what comes over the
pulpit. Your pastor seeks Me when he is writing His sermons. I give
Him words specifically for you. Grab them, delight in them, live

them. Take them seriously, as they come, straight from My throne, to you. You'll rejoice in the growth. You will be established and comforted, concerning the faith.

June 28

2 Thessalonians 2:2

That ye be not soon shaken in mind, or be troubled, neither by spirit, nor by word, nor by letter as from us, as that the day of Christ is at hand. KJV

Don't be troubled when you hear folks say, "Christ came and went," "Christ isn't coming again," "You've heard that for 2000 years, and he hasn't come yet." You will see the signs. You will know the truth. The truth will set you free of course. You just keep preaching the gospel of that truth and sharing the fact that Christ was born, died, and risen for them to have freedom from sin, forgiveness of sin. Share My plan of salvation through Calvary's cross. I want to give them resurrection power over their addictions, guilt and shame. They can bring their burdens to Me and I still deliver. And I am coming again. The world will attempt to shake you from these truths, stand firm in your faith.

June 29

Proverbs 29:9

If a wise man contendeth with a foolish man, whether he rage or laugh, there is no rest.   KJV

A sage trying to work things out with a fool gets only scorn and sarcasm for his trouble.   The Message

Many times, your sleeplessness night is only because of mind battles from the days decisions. I should have said..., I should have done..., I can't forget next time to...., and it spins on and on. This is why I tell you to stay as far from fools as possible. They will vex you and your rest. The sordidness of their behavior will affect you far beyond what you understand. They also will cause you to become ineffective for My kingdom. You have heard it said, you are who you hang with. There is a lot of truth in that statement. Be careful who you hang with. Love others, witness to many, but take care of yourself, be careful who you hang with, confide in, and trust. Check with Me when you are confused, chat with your headship, your pastor, your husband, find the clarity you need. I want you fit for the kingdom. We have your eternity at stake here.

June 30

Galatians 6:15

For in Christ Jesus neither circumcision availeth any thing, nor uncircumcision, but a new creature. KJV

Remember your first moments saved? Remember that awe? Return to that first love. That, my dear, is the new creature. Stand in awe. All of heaven rejoices over your salvation. You have no idea. We await your homecoming. You have much work to do yet on earth. I made you for a purpose. You have been ordained. You have been designed and set apart for kingdom purpose. We cheer you on. We envelope you, and fight when you fight. When you give up, you tie our hands. Keep that fighting spirit. Stand and we can move on your behalf. Sit and we cannot. This is warfare. A heavenly spiritual warfare. You can't see the wicked things you fight in high places. Let Me be your eyes on that. Follow Me. Pull out that sword of the Spirit. You got this!

July 1

1 John 2:29

Once you're convinced that he is right and righteous, you'll recognize that all who practice righteousness are God's true children.   The Message

If ye know that he is righteous, ye know that every one that doeth righteousness is born of him. KJV

If you cannot seem to do right, draw closer to Me. Fasting and prayer breaks many things. Fasting is a day with a little water, no food. Don't make a big show of it. It's no one else's business. You won't die. You'll live. Your flesh and its control over every facet of your life will die. There are some things that cannot be cast out but by prayer and fasting. And don't fast without prayer. That is just starvation. Pull down strongholds, out loud and with some passion in prayer. Don't live timidly. Live in confidence, and pray that way as well. I want to bring you some victories, some wins. Winners fight. Winners move. Winners do something. It takes action. Let's do this. I want to change the world and I want to start with you.

July 2

Proverbs 14:3

In the mouth of the foolish is a rod of pride; but the lips of the wise shall preserve them. KJV

In the mouth of the [arrogant] fool [who rejects God] is a rod for his back, But the lips of the wise [when they speak with godly wisdom] will protect them. AMP

Pride usually will show itself from the mouth. It speaks haughtiness and anger. It defends and cares nothing for those around it. The wise take care of what comes out of the mouth. Wisdom doesn't shoot off anger and undisciplined words causing hurt. Take time before you speak. Even if it is just a moment, it may change the entire course of someone around you. Slow to speak. It is unusual, but it will help you, it will help and preserve them as well.

July 3

2 Corinthians 3:17

..where the Spirit of the Lord is, there is liberty. KJV
..where the Spirit of the Lord is, there is freedom. ESV

Men long for freedom. They attempt to remove the shackles many ways. Their only true freedom comes by My Spirit. There is no victory without Christ. No other name is given to men but Jesus Christ, for salvation and freedom. Repent of your sin, ask Jesus into your heart, He will bring you freedom. And not that kind where you are just traded amongst this master or that one, one addiction taking the place of another. True freedom. That is what a life in Christ is all about. That's why He died such a horrible death and rose again. Just so you could taste freedom.

July 4

James 3:13-18

Who is a wise man and endued with knowledge among you? let him shew out of a good conversation his works with meekness of wisdom.

But if ye have bitter envying and strife in your hearts, glory not, and lie not against the truth.

This wisdom descendeth not from above, but is earthly, sensual, devilish.

For where envying and strife is, there is confusion, and every evil work.

But the wisdom that is from above is first pure, then peaceable, gentle, and easy to be entreated, full of mercy and good fruits, without partiality, and without hypocrisy.

And the fruit of righteousness is sown in peace of them that make peace.   KJV

You must treat others with dignity and honor. Most of the times this will not be a problem, many times it will. You must lean on Me in those times. How can a man be like Christ? How can a man react like Christ? Only through Christ in him. There is no other way. The huge challenge in your life is to get along with others. Do not twist the truth to make it seem you are ok. Be honest. Then I will honestly help you through this scenario. Remember always, look past them, see Me on the other side. This will give you strength to carry on.

This issue here is where many fall. I want you to get through it. Do not think this will be the last difficult person you will have to work with. There will be others as long as you walk upon the earth. However, I can teach you how to handle difficult people without degrading them and causing worse issues for you to deal with. Do not fear the cost, that will cause you to miss the blessing. Look up! I'm right here.

July 5

Philippians 1:6

Being confident of this very thing, that he which hath begun a good work in you will perform it until the day of Jesus Christ. KJV

When you pray, pick up your voice, pick up your face in confidence. Speak loudly, not muffled, let your petitions be made with all the confidence and faith you can find. Then watch Me move. Be specific. Then you will know it is an answer from Me. I want to move in your life. I want to be glorified through your prayers. Come on. You can do it! I love to use My people. I created you for this, and will astound you with the miracles you will see. People who see no miracles, no hand of God at work in their lives, aren't asking. You be different, you be the peculiar one. Let's go!

July 6

Psalms 93:5

Thy testimonies are very sure   KJV

When I left testimony behind in My Word it was so that you could have a picture of My abilities. Do not -- never ever -- discount any testimony in My Word. I placed them there for reference points for you to bear the difficult times, birth hope in your emotional situations, and be able to see a way out in the stressful circumstances, that this life will bring you. Mark it down, all these will come. My Word is the answer. Why? Because it teaches you who I am. When I say, "sup with me," I really mean that. Take time with Me during your coffee or your lunch, during down times, and breaks, before meetings or tests, early mornings and twilight evenings. Draw near to Me, and I will draw near to you. Open My Word, I will speak. Trust Me, I want to rock your world with resurrection power, to reach the lost and the dying.

July 7

Hebrews 2:3

How shall we escape, if we neglect so great salvation; which at the first began to be spoken by the Lord, and was confirmed unto us by them that heard him   KJV

Do not neglect this salvation that has been given to you. A high price was paid so that you may spend eternity with Me. Many times, if the man pays no price for the prize, the prize is tossed to the heap and not appreciated nor treasured, as the true gift and sacrifice of someone else's. Let this not be said of Mine, especially you. Look not to and fro for a better deal, an easier way. Trust Me with the road you are on, do not look back, no matter the struggle and the trial. I am right here with you. Nothing is too hard for Me. Allow these trials to mold and shape you. Look to Me. I have your back on this. The devil is a liar, you are so precious to Me. I prepare a place for you. If any of these things were not true, I would not have said them. Watch this page turn in your life, destiny is straight ahead, at the end of this road.

Galatians 6:13

All their talk about the law is gas. They themselves don't keep the law!   The Message

No human on earth can keep the law. I wrote it to show you your flaws and the need for a savior. Your Savior's name is Jesus. The only name given amongst men, whereby you must be saved. There is no other way into heaven but through the blood of My Son Jesus Christ. Many amongst you want you to follow this way and that way. Don't fall for it. They refuse My way because of hidden sin. They claim to know Me, yet do not do what I ask them to do. They spout bible verses but don't live them. They forbid you to eat pork, even meat, but are liars, thieves and adulterers, and flaunt it openly about you. Repent and be baptized. Seek a bible believing church that preaches the gospel. Tithe and support that church. Attend services faithfully. Love people. Give of yourself. Be in morning prayer, read the Word - so that I may direct you. These are not unusual requests. Nor unusual commands. This is your reasonable service and responsibility in My kingdom.

1 John 2:15-17

Don't love the world's ways. Don't love the world's goods. Love of the world squeezes out love for the Father. Practically everything that goes on in the world -- wanting your own way, wanting everything for yourself, wanting to appear important-- has nothing to do with the Father. It just isolates you from him. The world and

all its wanting, wanting, wanting is on the way out -- but whoever
does what God wants is set for eternity.   The Message

Love of Me is following My commandments. If you are confused
about them, take more time in the scriptures. I make them very plain,
only because I want you to understand and know them. I would not
write them to 'trip' you up or 'fool' you. I wrote them to rescue you.
If you can't hear My voice or My direction daily then take more time
to pray in the morning. I want you to hear and know My voice. I
have an incredible life and destiny for you, but you won't stumble
into it accidentally. It must be strategically fought for. Destiny and
eternity are tremendous things. The most important things in your
life. Only through Me will you have My perfect will in your life.

July 10

James 1:12

Blessed is the man that endureth temptation; for when he is tried,
he shall receive the crown of life, which the Lord hath promised to
them that love him.   KJV

Crown of life. You're going to want that. Jesus is the bread of life. I
will bring you life, and life more abundantly. Your goal is eternal
life, through Christ, who strengthens you. If you love Me, you will
keep My commandments, with a joy, not arguing about each one and
maybe do them, but begrudgingly. But follow as a child, following
His father's discipline and rules, without question. Just loving Father
enough to know, without a doubt, that his boundaries keep you from
harm. Trust Me. Love Me.

John 12:7-8

Let her alone; against the day of my burying hath she kept this.

For the poor always ye have with you; but me ye have not always.
KJV

Let her alone. She's anticipating and honoring the day of my burial. You always have the poor with you. You don't always have me. The Message

Judas was pretty wound up on how to spend someone else's money, wasn't he? He was also jealous of Christ. Jealous of the money of course but also of the attention he garnered. Judas was much like the religious zealots of that day. He even helped them to murder Christ. This is much the same as the religious spirit that operates in the earth today. They want to kill anything Jesus is doing. Many times, a move of God is mocked and ridiculed as too expensive, the money should go here. Many times, a move of God is attacked when it doesn't involve their ministry, but someone else's. Keep your heart right. Walk with Me. Praise and glorify My name when you see Me move, and always remember to love people. They have much to fight against in this world, one of their biggest obstacles is the religious spirit. They must have an example of others living for God. You must stay on course. Eyes forward. Think of Me. No matter what the world, religious or not, brings against you, eyes forward, think of Me. This is what Mary did. From Martha's scoldings to Lazarus' death to Judas' better ideas, she thought of Me. She loved Christ with all she had, all the time.

Psalms 104:19-23

The moon keeps track of the seasons, the sun is in charge of each day. When it's dark and night takes over, all the forest creatures come out. The young lions roar for their prey, clamoring to God for their supper. When the sun comes up, they vanish, lazily stretched out in their dens. Meanwhile, men and women go out to work, busy at their jobs until evening. The Message

Consider My wisdom. How I have set a pattern in order over all of the earth. Have you been, or met, the night time worker who refuses to work in my pattern? Their countenance is even affected. Their mind cannot grasp many truths. They walk dead and cannot see through the chaos. Consider My wisdom. Walk in it. I have laid a foundation of truths for your life. Morning prayer, meeting with Me, will begin a robust and beautiful day. Neglect it, neglect My patterns, neglect how I have created you to prosper, and you will fail. Plain and simple. Trust Me in this. Walk in Me, and you will prosper. Plain and simple.

John 12:49-50

For I have not spoken of myself; but the Father which sent me, he gave me a commandment, what I should say, and what I should speak.

And I know that his commandment is life everlasting; whatsoever I speak therefore, even as the Father said unto me, so I speak. KJV

Jesus spoke as I told Him. Do you? There are so many that walk all about you. I want you to talk to them about Me today. Awkward?, yes. Vital?, absolutely. You must break through your own uncomfortableness with people. You must. Bring that to Me. I will help you. Jesus was never comfortable. He separated many times to speak with Me about it. I helped Him. I will help you. They must hear My Word. They must. Be My voice. My Word truly is everlasting life, for you, for them. Tell them Jesus has the answers to their turmoil in life, whatever it may be, He wants to meet with them through a prayer of repentance. Remind them Jesus is real, a real savior, who died and rose again to give them victory over their struggles and pain. Be the one to speak to them today that Jesus loves them.

July 14

Galatians 6:9

And let us not be weary in well doing; for in due season we shall reap, if we faint not.   KJV

So let's not allow ourselves to get fatigued doing good. At the right time we will harvest a good crop if we don't give up, or quit.
The Message

The human body is designed to only extend itself so much. That is why you fatigue. Your strength must come from Me. Look up. Ask for My strength. I will give it to you abundantly. Remember- I am able - to do all things. And that includes strengthening Mine - especially for the work of My kingdom. Ask and you shall receive. Give and it shall be given back to you, pressed down, shaken together, overflowing. Need strength? Pray! Do things My way. It will make for a much easier burden. You will turn around in six months and be amazed at the accomplishments. The difference between the saints and the ain'ts is My strength and My grace - it truly is sufficient.

Galatians 5:4

Christ is become of no effect unto you, whosoever of you are justified by the law; ye are fallen from grace. KJV

You can absolutely never keep the entire law. That was the cause and need of the cross of Calvary and the blood that Christ shed. The resurrection power gives you the grace to become an overcomer. When you walk away from that grace and attempt to live by the law, you stumble from the grace, you fall from the grace. The law holds no freedom from sin, only discipline. However, those that preach the law, do not keep it themselves. They cannot. They are only human. Christ's effect in you, is mercy and grace. When you sin, repent and ask for forgiveness. His grace and mercy will flood your soul. That my friend, is resurrection power. That is Jesus Christ. You don't fall from grace, you run to it and embrace it with everything you got, and never let go.

July 16

Philippians 3:13-14

Brethren, I count not myself to have apprehended; but this one thing I do, forgetting those things which are behind, and reaching forth unto those things which are before,

I press toward the mark for the prize of the high calling of God in Christ Jesus. KJV

And a high calling it is. You are set apart. You are ordained. You have been called to much more than you are aware of. Your testimony alone, changes and impacts more people than you will ever know of on this side of heaven. When salvation through Jesus changes someone, the impact, by My design, is heard around the earth and all the way into heaven. Reach forward. Grow and change. Serve others. Love and strengthen those you are involved with. You will change the world. With Christ operating in and through you there can be no other result. As long as there is breath in your body, you will strive to change lives. When the breath leaves the body, your testimony will live on this earth even after you have departed.

July 17

Philippians 1:21

For to me to live is Christ, and to die is gain. KJV

Paul understood the need for the preaching of My gospel. He caught that revelation. Without someone to speak the words The Message is not received. As the deaf point to the ear and proclaim their deafness aloud, so also the sinner will point to their sin, out loud and without fear they will proclaim their hindrance from being able to hear My voice. Sin truly blocks their reception of Me. However, there are those who long to hear My Word. Who long to know of My forgiveness and grace. You must sift and seek the lost. You will find those who crave a touch of My hand. You will find those who cry out to Me in their darkness and emptiness of life. You want to be My servant? Do this. Seek the lost, speak My Word, and love people. Love them enough to pray and contend for them before My throne of grace. Life is short. Death is real.

July 18

Philippians 4:4-5

Rejoice in the Lord alway; and again I say, Rejoice.

Let your moderation be known unto all men. The Lord is at hand. KJV

Celebrate God all day, every day. I mean, revel in him! Make it as clear as you can to all you meet that you're on their side, working with them and not against them. Help them see that the Master is about to arrive. He could show up any minute!   The Message

When you rejoice in Me, the rest will fall into place. When Paul wrote the word 'moderation', he was asking the Philippians to let their testimony of their changed life through Christ shine before men. No longer excessively behaved as in arrogance and lack of self-control. This will cause you to be slower to react, slower to speak, which in turn displays unselfishness and consideration, able to forbear much more through tolerance towards others. Jesus is coming. He really is. This is all coming to a turning of the page for you and for My kingdom. Rejoice in Me, walk with Me, allow Me to change you, show others, and this will all prepare you. Eyes forward. Think of heaven!

July 19

Psalm 23:3

He restoreth my soul.   KJV

Restoration is an incredible thing. Take an old chair for instance. The seat can be worn through, with a leg loose or broken. It can be ugly to look at, many times discarded as not worth the trouble to 'fix' anymore. Ahh, but the master craftsman can take it into his hands and restore the beauty to the original intent of the creator of the piece. Rough finishes, from age and disrepair, are smoothed with great care. All the while keeping in mind the main goal is not to damage the wood. The shine, so dulled and lost by the wear and tear of the years of use and many times abuse, is brought back by the oil and the all-important touch of the master's hands.

I am that master. When I restore you, it is with My own hands. I love and care for you. Your soul is restored through salvation which brings rest, and the meeting of your needs. When going through trials, keep this in mind. The page will turn. You will not be discarded as old and used. You will get to the other side, and the restoring of your soul will be a refreshing thing. You will lie down in the green pastures. I will lead you to the still waters, and the paths of doing right, for My name, because you're mine. You won't need to fear evil, even though you are walking through the shadow of death, because I am here. I will comfort and keep you. Your enemies will see you, sitting at My table restored, your head anointed with oil, your cup filled. Goodness and mercy will be yours all the days of eternity, and you will dwell in My house, forever. All of this, because of restoration. I promise.

July 20

Proverbs 4:23

Keep your heart with all diligence; for out of it are the issues of life. KJV

You must guard your heart. It is easily corrupted by thoughts and attitude. No matter the circumstances, if your heart is right, it'll be ok. Ugliness comes out through bad attitude. What matters in your life is a heart that is right with Me. With a right heart, in the midst of turmoil you can be calm. Beware of the things that damage and break your heart. You will be betrayed in life. Betrayal many times tatters the heart. Also, being sidetracked by the things of this world. You will lose your first love for Me when you chase the trinkets of this world. Another danger is victimization. Calling yourself the victim, rather than being thankful in all circumstances. In everything give thanks. Don't allow the heart to grow hard, with unforgiveness towards others. Forgiveness is critical in guarding your heart. And then there's the defecting power of hidden sin. Sin rots the bones and encases the heart. You must repent of sin for it to be cleansed from your life. You must bring it to Me. A pure heart is what I seek. Like cleaning out your attic or basement. Open it before Me. I can help you pull out the muck and the filth. Your words expose your heart. Life and death are in the power of the tongue. When the heart is damaged, your words have the power to restore it. Speak life into your heart. In the midst of a heart stopping moment - David had to tell his heart to beat again. Take time. Guard your heart. Keep it for Me.

1 Samuel 30:6   David encouraged himself in the Lord his God.   KJV

July 21

Proverbs 3:3-4

Let not mercy and truth forsake thee: bind them about thy neck; write them upon the table of thine heart.

So shalt thou find favour and good understanding in the sight of God and man.   KJV

Don't lose your grip on Love and Loyalty. Tie them around your neck; carve their initials on your heart.

Earn a reputation for living well in God's eyes and the eyes of the people.   The Message

You long for favor with Me. You long for favor with others. This is how you find it. Love and loyalty - mercy and truth - you use these in dealing with folks and it will earn you a good reputation. When I can trust you with these, I can trust you with kingdom business. Think of them as tools for a carpenter. His project would come out unfinished, lopsided, uneven, unsafe and downright ugly, without the right tools. The tools give favor to the carpenter's hand. The carpenter's hand never becomes skilled without the correct tools. How would you trust a carpenter to build your home if he showed up without tools, or came in with gardening shears and a food processor? So also, you must show up with the correct tools.

Proverbs 25:16

Hast thou found honey? eat so much as is sufficient for thee, lest thou be filled therewith, and vomit it   KJV

Lack of self-control is a horrible thing. Ask Me. I need to help you with that. Fasting and prayer will be your victory over such things. Food is not the only thing you over-indulge in. Take time today and pray. Your spirit is willing; however, your flesh is weak. When you are unable to control in one area of the flesh, it is a signal that there are many areas that need attention paid to. As long as you're on this earth you will fight the flesh. A struggle with the flesh is an understatement. Fight the flesh is more realistic. Your flesh is huge compared to your spirit. But your hope is - My Spirit conquers all. This is your ace in the hole. I am able and so this makes you able. Call on Me. I will bring you victory. Fast and pray - this gives you the cutting edge. Far beyond your understanding.

Proverbs 25:17

When you find a friend, don't outwear your welcome; show up at all hours and he'll soon get fed up.   The Message

Withdraw thy foot from thy neighbor's house; lest he be weary of thee, and so hate thee.   KJV

Sometimes it's just time to go home. If you have no home, it's time to take care of that. Men and women are not designed to cohabitate outside of the marriage and family unit. This will lead to much aggravation and, well, hate. A dinner with someone is great. But when you refuse to leave when they are ready to rest, you wear on their hospitality. Don't do that to people. Find confidence and comfort in your own family or home. If you don't find it there, then it's time to address "why?" and rectify the situation. Build your nest. Guard your nest and keep it clean. Keep it clean physically of course, but spiritually as well. The mess in the spiritual might be the reason you can't keep it clean physically. Be willing to share. Love others. But you never have to allow someone to take over 'your' nest, especially when it is just because they are too lazy to build their own. Don't be too lazy to build 'your' own. That's your challenge. Make it comfortable. For you will need the rest - as well as your neighbor needs hers.

July 24

Psalm 91:11-12

He ordered his angels to guard you wherever you go. If you stumble, they'll catch you; their job is to keep you from falling. The Message

Psalm 91:14. I will set him on high, because he hath known my name. KJV

David knew My name. That is why I was able to set him on high. That is why angels were put in charge over him. If you know My name, draw close to Me. Meet with Me in the secret place. Cover yourself with My presence. Pray and contend until you know I am with you. Then My angels will guard you as well. Then you will be set on high also.

July 25

Proverbs 25:11

A word fitly spoken is like apples of gold in pictures of silver. KJV

Words are powerful. The spoken word goes far beyond anything you can understand. Guard what comes out of your mouth. You do not need to speak everything that pops into your head. Be very cautious and slow to speak in times of trial and temptation. You don't have to be a flatterer; however, the art of encouragement is a blessing to many. Encourage people. They get junk from so many others. Just love folks with your words and countenance. You'll change their day. You'll fill yours as well.

July 26

Psalm 104:3

Who walketh upon the wings of the wind.   KJV

You will do greater works because Jesus ascended back to heaven. You have so much potential. Do you not know of the Holy Spirit who resides within you? Stop and meditate on that. My Spirit dwells within you. Your members, your heart, your spirit are all covered and inhabited by Me. You can do all things. Take time and pray, meditate on these things. Then go conquer that world which troubles you. I have already overcome it. Pray for the sick. Preach deliverance and set at liberty those who are captives. Walk in that today. You got this!

July 27

God is my defense

Psalm 59:9

Because of his strength will I wait upon thee: for God is my defence.   KJV

My strength is so much more than you realize. I want to give you a glimpse of it. Read the psalm again.

Psalm 59:16

But I will sing of thy power   KJV

The psalmist understood. When you forget, take time in the psalms. I gave the psalmist many revelations of my character, mostly for you to read today, from a book written so long ago. I wanted to speak to you. I wanted to remind you of My strength and power, and that it is all available to you - to give you the victory over this world. When you read the word 'power', do you see it? Do you understand it? Take time and ponder on it. The 'power' of an 'almighty' God is at your disposal. Trust Me. That's what I love. When you trust Me, just as a child does his father, trust Me, just because you can, just because you're mine, that My friend - is relationship.

July 28

Psalms 94:14

For the Lord will not cast off his people, neither will he forsake his inheritance.   KJV

I have promised you many things. Can the human mind grasp them all? Ahh, but I will not forget. My promises are true. Consider Abraham. He is not even alive on the earth with you to see all of the promises I have kept to him and his inheritance. But I keep them. So, you must trust Me as well. Abraham believed Me. That is a fact. He just believed Me when I spoke. Do you? When pondering My promises to you, remember I have a plan. My promises are part of them. You are more important to Me than you realize. I will not forget. Walk in Me while I mold and shape your destiny.

Psalm 143:8

Cause me to hear thy lovingkindness in the morning; for in thee do I trust; cause me to know the way wherein I should walk; for I lift up my soul unto thee. KJV

If you wake me each morning with the sound of your loving voice, I'll go to sleep each night trusting in you. The Message

Need an uplift of soul? Come to Me. Trust Me when I speak. You will hear Me. Draw close. Ask Me to show you things. I will blow you away with responses. Many times, immediately. Many times, through a thought or someone else during your day. But I'll answer. I want you to get to know the different ways I speak. But you'll know it's Me. Ask Me peculiar questions that no one else would know you asked. Pray specifically for things instead of generally. Than it can be more obvious to you - that I am answering. Let Me make myself real to you. You need to know My voice, so you can react in confidence.

July 30

Psalm 144:1

Blessed be the Lord my strength which teacheth my hands to war, and my fingers to fight   KJV

When I call you to do things - many times the enemy comes with a direct frontal attack. Other times it is much more subdued. He will use family and friends to speak things. He will mess with your mind and spirit. Consider David on the battlefield with Goliath vs. Eve being cunningly beguiled by the serpent. You must be prayed up. Fasting will also expose many things in the spiritual realm you wouldn't normally see or notice. Read My Word so I can use it - as it is living and becomes embedded in you as you nourish yourself in it - so I can use it to rescue you from evil. Put on My whole armor, not just a piece of it. David never went out without his sword. Your sword is the Spirit, which is My Word. David never took aim without first equipping his feet, so you equip yours with the gospel of peace. David could never have won without girding his loins, gird yours with truth. When the enemy came on the battlefield against him he would have had no chance without his breastplate, yours should be of righteousness. How would he quench the fiery darts of hell without his shield of faith held high, polished and gleaming in the sun! You must, like him, remember your helmet of salvation, that is also My Word. My Word is critical to your surviving! Never let it go. Dig deep, dive in, every single day of your life. When David left the battlefield and went home, he allowed someone else to fight his battles, he took off his armor, and as it fell by the wayside - he fell - headlong into sin and failure. Always remember to stay - fight your battles! Always remember to keep your armor on! That's why I've equipped you, because it's needed.

July 31

1 Thessalonians 5:24
Faithful is he that calleth you, who also will do it. KJV

The One who called you is completely dependable. If he said it, he'll do it! The Message

Remember in life that you can always count on Me, your Father, your Creator. I have created you for a specific purpose. I am molding and shaping you daily for that purpose. If it wasn't so, I wouldn't have called you nor promised you. I do not lie. Trust Me. This helps Me move in your life. I have tied hands, muted lips, bound feet, when you will not trust Me. Move forward with Me, as I have called you. Watch what I do, you'll be amazed and changed. Let go and let Me turn this page.

August 1

Psalm 144:1-2

Blessed be God, my mountain, who trains me to fight fair and well. He's the bedrock on which I stand, the castle in which I live, my rescuing knight, the high crag where I run for dear life, while he lays my enemies low.   The Message

Many times, in life you refuse to recognize your enemy. This is a gracious thing most of the time, and needs to happen. But sometimes when they steal your joy, victory, and what you need to be accomplishing for Me -- well then that's another story. Ask Me when they bring you down, or tend to tromp all over you and where I've placed you. Take dominion. Do not allow that. Every place your foot stands has dominion. Never forget that. I had dominion at the cross. I had it! Not them. I had to allow the circumstances for the outcome. That's ministry. So sometimes things do not seem fair. But I will always give you the upper hand. Look for My will in all things. The art of ministry is My will in the circumstance. I'm going to show you somethings today. Trust Me. I'm right here.

August 2

Proverbs 2:1-22

if thou wilt receive my word..   KJV

I will be a personal body guard to the candid and sincere. I pay special attention to My loyally committed ones, and preserve the way of My saints.

Wisdom, knowledge, discretion and understanding are critical in your life.

I will use them to deliver you from:

the ones who left

the ones who walk in darkness

the ones who rejoice in doing evil

the ones who delight in wickedness

the ones who forgot the covenant of God

their house and their paths are dead.

The upright and the perfect will dwell in My land forever and never leave. The women of integrity will last.

(Paraphrased from The Message)

My promises never return void or incomplete. There's a big 'if' here. 'If' you will receive My Word. Receive, without arguing with it. Treasure it as a manual for life. Hold it close as personal correspondence with Me. Then you will run straight into and with understanding, wisdom, knowledge and discretion. It's a kingdom principle. Grasp it. The world will always leave you empty and wanting. Let Me fill your life.

August 3

Colossians 3:12-13

Put on therefore, as the elect of God, holy and beloved, bowels of mercies, kindness, humbleness of mind, meekness, longsuffering; Forbearing one another and forgiving one another.   KJV

So, chosen by God for this new life of love, dress in the wardrobe God picked out for you:

> *compassion,*
>
> *kindness,*
>
> *humility,*
>
> *quiet strength,*
>
> *discipline.*

Be even-tempered, content with second place, quick to forgive an offense. Forgive as quickly and completely as the Master forgave you. And regardless of what else you put on, wear love. It's your basic, all-purpose garment. Never be without it.   The Message

I know your concern is your closet. What will fit today. What will look good today. Driven by mood. Driven by temper. Driven by circumstances of course. I challenge you to a spiritual wardrobe.

Needed in every season of life. Fits any body shape or weight, even yours, even if you consumed more than you should have of that Mexican food last night. It always looks good on you. It never goes out of style. I always will say, "you look great in that." Let's review it again.

Mercies

Kindness

Humbleness of mind

Meekness

Longsuffering

Forbearance

Forgiveness

And always, always, always remember - that go to outfit? - love. LOVE. It looks awesome on you every time. I never get tired of seeing you in that. Ask Me if you have trouble finding it. I'll help.

August 4

Proverbs 4:26-27

Ponder the path of thy feet, and let all thy ways be established.

Turn not to the right hand nor to the left; remove thy foot from evil. KJV

Watch your step, and the road will stretch out smooth before you. Look neither right nor left; leave evil in the dust. The Message

Many run to and fro trying to figure out what to do. 'Mine' ponder the path, take their time in the morning to allow Me to direct their steps, and find rest at the end of their full and accomplished day. No matter the chaos of life, they carry on. Why? Because I show and teach Mine how to walk. Think of it like this. That forest lane. It has been taken over and over by many throughout the years. It is well traveled. It is well worn. Many a traveler has decided on that way because of the ease of the walk. However, had it not been for the first travelers walking and using the lane, the others would never have walked it. Those early travelers made the path straight so that they could find their way the next time. They pondered it and worked it out. And it was straight. That is why others came along and with no thought walk along it and expect it to lead to safety through safe areas - only because it is now well worn and frequently used. I want to make your path straight. I want to lighten your burden. I want you to follow Me. Ponder in the morning. Find the straight path. That one that no matter what comes along it, you know there is safety on it and at the end of it. This will establish your ways.

August 5

1 Peter 5:8

Be sober, be vigilant; because your adversary the devil, as a roaring lion, walketh about, seeking whom he may devour; KJV

Keep a cool head. Stay alert. The devil is poised to pounce, and would like nothing better than to catch you napping. Keep up your guard. You're not the only ones plunged into these hard times. It's the same with Christians all over the world. So keep a firm grip on the faith. The Message

Sometimes you will be called to face the lion, the enemy. I am your deliverer. You know I laid the Red Sea open. The only reason I did that was to rescue my people. And when I did, they stared straight at it and knew it was Me. When you face the lion, I am there. Right next to you. I see him. I see you. I deliver. Watch out for folks in the meantime. When you are going through the fire, the testing, be very careful how you treat others. You are not the only one. Leaders keep an eye out for the others. Don't kill them. Share some of the compassion I have taught you about. As my people walked straight through a sea, they went together. They had victory together. Not one was lost. Some were fearful and lacking in faith. Others were full of faith and ready to roll with Me. I wanted them all. I got them all. Take a look about you. Bring as many as you can through and out of these trying times. Be kind, especially to other Christians. They take enough ugly from the world. You show them beauty, from Me.

August 6

Psalms 35:27

... Let the Lord be magnified, which hath pleasure in the prosperity of his servant. KJV

When you struggle and can't seem to make ends meet, know that I am there willing to lend the hand. Look up, speak to Me, and then pay attention and do what I tell you to do. Think for a moment, if Jesus would not have asked for the boy's lunch. Where would the miracle be? If the boy, who by the way was not well to do, had not shared it? What of the widow of Zarepath? You will never, ever see a miracle in your life without obedience. It ties my hands. So, look up, ask and receive. But remember to receive the instructions of where to find it, silly. So many miss it, because they won't quit sulking in their room, and come out to find and look and see what I have done. Go now, take that land, it's yours.

August 7

Psalms 126:5-6

They that sow in tears shall reap in joy.

He that goeth forth and weepeth, bearing precious seed, shall doubtless come again with rejoicing, bringing his sheaves with him. KJV

There is such power and potential in the seed. More than you comprehend. You speak, even in prayer to Me, "if you would make it fruitful, I would spread more of your Word." Know you not that some will plant, others water, and still others reap. You just spread it. Leave the reaping to Me. That's the way it works. It doesn't take rocket science to understand this. However, it does take faith. You know very well that folks like a return on their investment and time, immediately. But you are not to live by the world's economy, nor by its expectations. Look at the hull of a seed. Who could expect a huge harvest from such a creation. Only I see the end of the seed you plant. Remember this when sharing My Word. My Word changes people. My Word builds. It also convicts and chips away at flesh and hardness of heart and sin that has built up over the years in a human life. You are called to sow the Word. I bring the growth. Everything with Me begins with a seed. You will reproduce after your own kind. I am not interested in counterfeits. The seed you sow will release a harvest. Fruitfulness comes to those who love what they have and are thankful for where I have placed them.

John 15:16 Ye have not chosen me, but I have chosen you, and ordained you, that ye should go and bring forth fruit, and that your fruit should remain; that whatsoever ye shall ask of the Father in my name, he may give it you.   KJV

August 8

Mark 4:14, 19

The sower soweth the Word.

And the cares of this world, and the deceitfulness of riches, and the lusts of other things entering in, choke the word, and it becometh unfruitful. KJV

If fruitfulness can't be aborted from the inside, hell will try to choke it from the outside. There is a demonic stalker that is after your destiny. There is a predator tracking you. Jesus named the stalkers. Look at them. Familiarize yourself with them. Beware of them. That is why Jesus spoke it. Are you caring about things that you aren't designed to carry? Do your worries of the day choke out your time with Me?, your faith in Me? Are you so concerned with your 'to do' list, that you do not even consult Me to see if that is what I would have you do today? Do the 'things and stuff' you long to acquire distract you from even Sunday services now? Does your stress strangle what you do hear, when you do hear My Word, so nothing comes of it? Take time in morning prayer and talk to Me about these things. I will help you sort it out. Embrace My Word, quit discounting it. I want to help you grow and I want to help you to be fruitful in My Kingdom.

Mark 4:20

But the seed planted in the good earth represents those who hear the Word, embrace it, and produce a harvest beyond their wildest dreams. The Message

August 9

Ecclesiastics 9:17-18

The quiet words of the wise are more effective

Than the ranting of a king of fools.

Wisdom is better than warheads,

But one hothead can ruin the good earth. The Message

Whenever you realize you are ranting, stop and pray. Mine do not rant. Mine speak with a quiet wisdom. It's much more effective. People who rant speak without thinking. Don't speak off the top of your head. Take a 3 second break, at least, to speak. Especially when it is a situation that is heated. You may not control warheads, however, your influence in people's lives - it is far more than you realize. Build them, don't destroy them. Words are powerful. They cannot be taken back.

August 10

Where the Spirit of the Lord is there is freedom.

2 Corinthians 3:17

Where the spirit of the Lord is, there is liberty.   KJV

2 Corinthians 3:18

And so we are transfigured much like the Messiah, our lives gradually becoming brighter and more beautiful as God enters our lives and we become like him. The Message

Where My Spirit is there is freedom. The rock-solid foundation of Jesus Christ is where your salvation rests. That is where it comes from. The law exposed your sin. The law revealed - and it needed to be revealed - because it had you blinded - revealed your sin to you. I didn't need to have it revealed. You did. This is why the law was. This is why Christ died. After the revelation of the sin in your life that separates you from Me, you realized the need for a Savior. As you surrendered your life to Christ, I was able to begin the transformation of your life to be more like Me. As you grow, you become more and more transfigured revealing the light of Christ, and this becomes the beauty as well. You now have freedom. Where My Spirit dwells, there is freedom.

Job 11:13-19

"Still, if you set your heart on God and reach out to him,

If you scrub your hands of sin and refuse to entertain evil in your home,

You'll be able to face the world unashamed and keep a firm grip on life, guiltless and fearless.

You'll forget your troubles; they'll be like old, faded photographs.

Your world will be washed in sunshine, every shadow dispersed by dayspring.

Full of hope, you'll relax, confident again; you'll look around, sit back, and take it easy.

Expansive, without a care in the world, you'll be hunted out by many for your blessing.

The Message

You long for the safety and rest to settle your mind from all fears and frustrations. May I remind you, rest in Me. In the midst of the storms, in the center of the chaos, Mine stand firm and relaxed and comfortable. They sleep soundly when their body needs rest. They smile when others fret and pout. They generally laugh and find victory in all of their circumstances. Yes, sometimes they need a moment to process the situation. Ah, but, it is all how they process it that counts. Process it through Me. I want to take your troubles and replace them with a lightened burden. Let Me bless you with My presence. Then nothing but blessing and grace will chase you. You don't chase blessings, remember. They will chase you.

2 Corinthians 3:16

Whenever, though, they turn to face God as Moses did, God removes the veil and there they are -- face to face! They suddenly recognize that God is a living, personal presence, not a piece of chiseled stone. The Message

As I entered your life, the challenge was settled. Will you continue to surrender all? Remember when you were a new convert? It seemed such a pleasure to you to give Me all. You met Me face to face, so childlike. Ready to face the world trusting My decisions. As the years have gone by you have been challenged far beyond what you ever could have imagined. And look how you have grown. Strong in the faith. Yet now that I ask you to take a step into this unknown task, you seem apprehensive even to yourself. Open your heart. I got this too. Speak words of faith. It will change your apprehension into a joy and expectancy for this next adventure to unfold. I will repeat My promise to you. Just for a reminder. I will never leave you, nor forsake you. I will never give you more than you can handle. What seems insurmountable is usually My request. Ask Gideon. I am not a stone, unable to speak and challenge you. I am not an idol where you lay your requests and expect Me to not hear nor move. I have heard you. I still design your destiny. Take a leap of faith. Speak it into existence. Speak as if it was. Even before you see the evidence. Just because I've asked. No other reason.

August 13

Psalms 96:11-13
Let's hear it from Sky,
With Earth joining in,
And a huge round of applause from Sea.

Let Wilderness turn cartwheels,

Animals, come dance,

Put every tree of the forest in the choir --

An extravaganza before God as he comes,

As he comes to set everything right on earth,

Set everything right, treat everyone fair.   The Message

Nature is an amazing thing. It rolls My way at a whisper of My voice. I made it to enthrall you. I made it to build you. There are storms of course. Many storms are necessary to refurbish and revitalize the earth and its creatures. This includes man. This includes you. It usually seems only the strong survive. But look closer. I am building and making the weak - stronger, the strong - wiser. I am always causing growth. No one leaves - life - without My permission. It is appointed unto man once to die, and then the judgment. Trust Me in all things. I got this. I am Creator of all things. You are My workmanship. Allow Me access to build you. I never violate your will. Pray. Draw close. Ask Me to help you align your will with Mine. Nature doesn't ask. I command it. With you, the covenant is much deeper. It is relationship I want with you.

August 14

<u>Top o the morning to you</u>

Proverbs 8:34-35

Blessed is the man that heareth me, watching daily at my gates, waiting at the posts of my doors. For whoso findeth me findeth life, and shall obtain favor of the Lord. KJV

Blessed the man, blessed the woman, who listens to me, awake and ready for Me each morning, alert and responsive as I start my day's work. When you find me, you find life, real life, to say nothing of God's good pleasure. The Message

If you will begin your day with Me, your Creator, your day would begin with My presence. My presence is what heals and restores and prepares you for your day's battles. As a soldier does not forget his boots, do not forget Me. How else would mine clad themselves for the most basic protections of the day? How else would mine find the correct path? Without boots, you would naturally choose the easy path all the day long. You must be prepared for the rough roads ahead. How else would mine prevail? Meet with Me. Take time with Me. Wait on Me. And My presence shall transform you every single day.

August 15

2 Samuel 24:24

And the king said .... neither will I offer burnt offerings unto the Lord my God of that which doth cost me nothing.   KJV

....No, I've got to buy it from you for a good price; I'm not going to offer God, my God, sacrifices that are no sacrifice.   The Message

When you realize, "but, when I repented it cost me nothing," then you will be more willing to realize the privilege to pay the price in serving God. Serving Me is ministry. At last you will be able to enjoy the fruits of your labor.

Many are called, few are chosen. Few finish the race, although many run the course for a while. Do not grow weary in well doing. Well doing is your life line to Christ. How else shall they be won to Christ? Seek and you shall find, find that strength in My presence.

Ask Me for help. I long to move in your life and help you finish your course.

August 16

When I Am Falling

Isaiah 40:27-31

Why would you ever complain, O Jacob, or whine, Israel, saying, "God has lost track of me. He doesn't care what happens to me"? Don't you know anything? Haven't you been listening? God doesn't come and go. God lasts. He's Creator of all you can see or imagine. He doesn't get tired out, doesn't pause to catch His breath. And He knows everything, inside and out. He energizes those who get tired, gives fresh strength to dropouts. For even young people tire and drop out, young folk in their prime stumble and fall. But those who wait upon God, get fresh strength. They spread their wings and soar like eagles, they run and don't get tired, they walk and don't lag behind. The Message

When you are falling, or the pressures of life come, and it just feels like you are falling, under these testings, take time to cry to Christ. Where else would you go? In your circumstances of life, you have burnt so many bridges. Family has left your side, many friends, as they have drifted away from the things of Me, no longer seem concerned of your well-being today. It is always interesting to Me how the conversations with these 'old' friends is always on their 'old' wounds and not their present victories. Many times, this frustrates your soul, and you see no reason to spend time with them. Distractions come in and your lack of interest keeps you from sharing the gospel with them. You need to overcome this area of your life. Your confidence and strengths in times of pressure because of your hope in Christ draws these people continually to you. It is because of your testimony of a victorious life through all circumstances that shines a bright light towards them and beckons them. They are curious. They need direction but many times are too prideful to ask. Be slow to speak and handle them carefully, these are souls I have led to you. Pray for strength and energy and then give them hope through Christ. It is quite a challenge, but you are up to it.

August 17

<u>People Matter</u>

1 Peter 1:6-7

I know how great this makes you feel, even though you have to put up with every kind of aggravation in the meantime. Pure gold put in the fire comes out of it proved pure; genuine faith put through this suffering comes out proved genuine. When Jesus wraps this all up, it's your faith, not your gold, that God will have on display as evidence of His victory. The Message

...your faith .. more precious than gold ... KJV

In these days of "black lives matter" demonstrations, be reminded how far away the world and its human occupants have fallen from Christ's original sacrifice. He died for all. This was My original plan. Remember I created all? As the world wants to decide that they are gods and hold life and death in their own hands, i.e. abortions of innocent human lives, death panels to decide who gets medical care and who is not worth it, assisted suicide protection laws where folks are left free to deride their family members into believing that their life is no longer precious to anyone, and the list goes on all the way to wars, man-made chemicals to destroy humans and their foods; they have forgotten- I am still in control. So many times, in history man thought they had it all figured out, just ask Hitler. So many times, in life 'You' thought you had it all figured out. You did not. Nor does anyone else. Your life and times on this earth are all here to mold and shape you for an eternity with Christ. You certainly don't understand all of this. You still believe that I do. Remember the illustration of the great carpet in the sky. From your point of view, it is the backside of the carpet. A mess of knots and string and threads out of place. On the other side, from up above, My side, it is a beautiful tapestry, luscious colors flowing together, each stitch in place, solidly in place, for eternity, never to unravel or fade away. Long for a look at that tapestry. That eternity. That destiny. That destiny includes you. Ask Me - 'Bend me Lord. I need it today. Mold me and shape me, I need you so'.

August 18

Follow Him

1 Samuel 25:40-41

Then David sent for Abigail to tell her that he wanted her for his wife. David's servants went to her at Carmel with The Message, "David sent us to bring you to marry him." She got up, and then bowed down, face to the ground, saying, "I'm your servant, ready to do anything you want. I'll even wash the feet of my master's servants." The Message

...let thine handmaid be a servant... KJV

Do you recall the spoiled child you saw with her mother? Do you recall your disdain for the both of them as she ranted and raved for what she wanted and refused to heed the pleadings and directions of her parent? Do you recall the darling little one you saw, who spoke politely, used manners, and even opened the door for his elders, with a joy in his heart? Not out of anything but habit, evidence of what his father had taught him? So, I teach over and over to you. Many lessons appear repetitious. How else would My child learn how to react as a Christian, a child of God, lest he be taught. So that it is a natural part of him. Obedience, serving, good heart, kindness, all of the fruits of the Spirit, should be a natural part of My child's life. As you master one, I am able to move on to the next lesson, bringing a maturity and stamina to your walk in Christ.

August 19

Job 23:10

....when He hath tried me, I shall come forth as gold.   KJV

When gold is put through the fire the dross comes to the top. This is a process of purity. When I try and test you, take a good look at what comes out of you. Look at your attitudes, the words you speak, the feeling you have inside of you. This is the dross in your life. This is what needs to surface so that it can be dealt with. You deal with it through repentance and contending in prayer in the supernatural to rid your life of it. Deal with it now, as it exposes itself, and you will see great growth and victories in your life. Bury it, and I will bring you back through trials to surface it again until you get a handle on it. I don't mind bringing you back where you started from to work some things out of you. I want the pure you to come forth like gold. Remember Jonah was spit out by a whale on the same beach he left from when he refused to obey me. I had to return him to that beach to give him that same opportunity to get things right. He did not look like gold covered in fish spit. However, I was able to use him for a great revival as a result of simple street preaching.

August 20

Psalms 42:5

...He puts a smile on my face, He's my God ....   The Message

...hope thou in God...   KJV

It's been a long road, or so it seems to you, on this earth. I have much planned for you. Many blessings, many twists and turns of trials and testing. You already understand these are to build not destroy. To strengthen you, not to weaken. You will overcome, because you continue to put your hope in Me. As you walk this journey, as you see the obstacles, take time to worship, take time to pray, ask for My help. Lean not on your own understanding and supplies. I will bring you through quickly. Train your eye and heart on Me. This will make your burden light and bring rest to your soul and yes, a smile to your face. I will place it there.

August 21

<u>Pretty Feet</u>

Isaiah 52:7

"How beautiful on the mountains are the feet of the messenger bringing good news, Breaking the news that all's well, proclaiming good times, announcing salvation, telling Zion, "Your God reigns!" Voices! Listen! Your scouts are shouting, thunderclap shouts, shouting in joyful unison. They see with their own eyes GOD coming back to Zion. Break into song! Boom it out, ruins of Jerusalem: " GOD has comforted his people! He's redeemed Jerusalem!" GOD has rolled up his sleeves. All the nations can see his holy, muscled arm. Everyone, from one end of the earth to the other, sees him at work, doing his salvation work." The Message

Thy God reigneth.. KJV

I have seen your labors in my name. I have watched you toil and spin and continually cry out for strength. As you do this, I have met you. You have seen many pages in your life lift and turn. This is how you have seen the victories. As you place your worn foot in front of the other, even when it seems you cannot, I have met you there and won the victory. There is much left to do on this earth as I mold and shape your destiny. Stay on that road. Witness of Me, share My hope, be kind because of Me. Take time on purpose, for others. Follow your leadership, fast and pray. Victory is Mine, and also yours.

2 Chronicles 7:14

If my people, which are called by my name, shall humble themselves, and pray, and seek my face, and turn from their wicked ways; then will I hear from heaven, and will forgive their sin, and will heal, their land.   KJV

Many come, many call My name, many check their humility at the door. Humbleness is an amazing thing. When someone comes to you - requesting something - if they come in high minded and demanding - are you able to give it freely as compared to the person who comes -subdued, humiliated, under subjection? Humbleness is not a game or show, it is a condition of the heart that shows and displays itself in the countenance of men and women. Humble people do pray, they seek My face, they turn away from wickedness as they turn to Me. This frees Me to hear, to forgive your sin, which opens the door for your land to be healed as well. Never underestimate the power of your prayers. I hear them. There are many things that happen when you pray. Continue to contend. Your prayers are a wonderful aroma to Me in the morning. Thank you.

James 5:16

The effectual fervent prayer of a righteous man availeth much.
KJV

James could say this because he experienced this with Me. They called James 'camel knees'. He spent a lot of time on those knees - meeting with Me. How much time do you spend? You say you have urgent prayers. You speak that to others, but you do not urgently present these things to Me. You tell others, "I'm praying for you." And you do - but do you fervently pray? You expect mountains moved. It is time you moved them. Prayer is an action. Prayer is a labor. Prayer is not just fancy sounding words. Prayer is engaging against spiritual wickedness in high places, through Christ Jesus who strengthens you. Why does Jesus strengthen you? Because you need strength when you pray. Do not meet with Me as the religious do, for show and pomp, and their own glory. Meet with Me for action to take place. Run with Me on this. I have a plan -- it is to fulfill your destiny. Come, have some zeal in obtaining it.

August 24

Deuteronomy 33:25

Thy shoes shall be iron and brass; and as thy days, so shall thy strength be. KJV

...his feet massaged in oil.

Safe behind iron-clad doors and gates, your strength like iron as long as you live. The Message

As thy days, so shall your strength be. Your strength is like iron clad doors and gates. Your protection in My strongholds are like none known on the earth. I am your strength, your rest, I am your security. When you are going through hard times, they are to humble and build you, not to hurt you. They are to teach you how to cry out to Me, lean on Me, and find your strength in Me. They are to build and form you, shape you into who you are called to be. They are to prove you, to do you good at the latter end. You do not find strength by bread alone, but by every Word that proceeds out of My mouth. Look at the children of Israel in the desert. For 40 years I humbled and suffered them, and fed them with manna. Their clothes never got old, their feet never swelled. I chastened them as a Father does his child. But there was the promise. The dream if you will. You have dreams. I have given you promises. Always with the dream, or promise, or word, is the high in life. Then turn the page, here comes the challenge stage, or the death and burial stage. Perseverance, learning to trust Me, this is what is built in that stage. Then flip the page again, the promise is realized. Is there nothing like hope realized at the end that seems so amazing after the perseverance. Some would call this the resurrection stage. Without the proving it is so much easier to forget - who fed thee in the wilderness with manna, who brought water out of a rock to quench your thirst, who led you through that wilderness, who brought all of these blessings into your life after all. Do not forget Me on the other side of the trial. It's all a stepping stone to your destiny. There is so much more to come. You still need Me, never forget that, lest you stumble and fall.

August 25

Psalm 104:4

Who maketh his angels spirits; his ministers a flaming fire. KJV

A minister is an ambassador of My Word. Folks on this earth need to hear so they can do. What do they need to hear? The evening news? The latest health tips? They seek and listen to these, however, what they need to hear is My Word. You are My ambassador. In order to speak it so it is heard above the rabble and the discourse of their day you must be set ablaze with a flaming fire. The fire only burns in one that is filled with the Holy Spirit, this is the oil and the fuel, if you will. You want to make a difference in this earth. You long and cry for fruitfulness. Pray for the Holy Ghost to fill you up and overflowing. I can do that. But you must pray and contend for it. You must live clean and set aside. You must love right and hate evil. I need a clean vessel to fill. Come on! Let's get on this! Go and tell someone I have come to set them free through the blood of Christ.

Hebrews 1:14 Are they not all ministering spirits, sent forth to minister for them who shall be heirs of salvation? KJV

Matthew 25:46

And these shall go away into everlasting punishment: but the righteous into life eternal. KJV

Eternity is real. Hell is real. Heaven is real. Heaven is beyond the imagination of the human mind. You have never seen nor heard the things that await you in heaven. The righteous will see God. The righteous will walk with God. The righteous live by faith in this earth. Spend time with Me. Spend time in the Word. This fuels your faith. How can one have faith in another if there is no relationship? If we did not speak to each other how would there be a relationship? I am not a dumb statue that I do not speak. Open My Word, speak to Me. Then listen. I speak. I will meet with you in so many ways that it will delight your soul and ignite your faith.

August 27

Ezekiel 12:28

Thus saith the Lord God; There shall none of my words be prolonged any more, but the word which I have spoken shall be done, saith the Lord God. KJV

There comes a time of fulfillment of My promises to My promised. I have promised you many things. When Ezekiel spoke these words, and recorded them for Me, I was speaking to a rebellious generation. As you live in this rebellious generation, surrounded by disobedience, do not be alarmed at the judgments you will endure along with them, only because you are amongst them. I will cover you though. Do not fear as you see the end days prophecies appear to unfold. Do not fear as the heathen or the unfaithful religious world does. Look up. It is only more evidence for you that your redemption is soon. Trust Me. I make promises, and I keep them. Continue to contend in prayer for your generation. There is much spiritual warfare at hand. Never ever ever quit. Eternity is at hand.

August 28

Philippians 4:8

Finally brethren, whatsoever things are true, whatsoever things are honest, whatsoever things are just, whatsoever things are pure, whatsoever things are lovely, whatsoever things are of good report; if there be any virtue, and if there be any praise, think on these things. KJV

I want to bless your life. Speak words of blessing. Allow Me to move through the spoken word in your life. Tuck the negative things aside and let Me take care of them. Keep your mind and especially your words on the good things, the lovely things. It will help you to not only stay saved, but also to enjoy your walk in Christ. Pick yourself up out of the gloomy glooms of your day, through those words you speak and allow Me to change your countenance through the Word of your God.

August 29

2 Corinthians 5:13-14

If I acted crazy, I did it for God. ...

Christ's love has moved me to such extremes. The Message

If we are out of our mind ... it is for God.

for the love of Christ controls and compels us. AMP

For whether we be beside ourselves, it is to God: or whether we be sober, it is for your cause.

For the love of Christ constraineth us ... KJV

Paul loved to respond when I asked him to write My church for Me. Sometimes he had to explain his own zeal. His zeal was beyond words. He did act crazy sometimes. He was called to act sober other times. But My love for him constrained him and helped him. My love also moved him. Without a love for Me and a love from Me - moving you- your efforts are foolish. With the love involved, the relationship with Me, My will for your life - today - involved, you will be moved to crazy actions - sober actions - actions that will be called - out of your mind - but they will be of Me. Trust Me to constrain and also to compel you. Without action, interaction with others, your life is ineffective. Get involved with people. It will drive you crazy sometimes. Sometimes you will over react. But you'll never win a soul nor make an impact unless you step out into this arena. Trust Me to move you to such extremes. It's what it's all about.

August 30

Hebrews 11:6

For without faith it is impossible to please him; for he that cometh to God must believe that he is, and that he is a rewarder of them that diligently seek him. KJV

It's impossible to please God apart from faith. And why? Because anyone who wants to approach God must believe both that he exists and that he cares to respond to those who seek him.
The Message

Whoever comes near to Me, must believe I exist. When those folks approach that don't believe I 'can' help, that I am unable to assist, well - My hands are tied. Faith is the key to the miracle. The size of a mustard seed, My friend. The size of a mustard seed, give it to Me, and I will move your mountains. Gone, they will be gone. But I must have faith - from you! Remember the widow with the two mites offering? Jesus was excited. Why was He excited? Because it was the key where I could be able to bless that woman after many fervent prayers of hers. I take note of your life. I see. I know. I press and deal with you. I speak and answer prayer. I dealt with that woman to throw in her last mites. And she did. That, My friend, moved her mountain, her obstacles, the things that kept her in poverty. That's why Jesus was excited. I want to bless. I love to bless. You must live your life with a confidence and belief in My promises and also in the direction I am bringing you. Respond how and where I want you to. Give give give. Not just your money. Give your words to someone today. Give your hope. Give your patience. Give your kindness. Pass a tract. Love somebody. Come out of your shell. There are so many to reach. I need you to be My hands and feet. Walk in faith. As you respond, so will I. Your situation can and will change if you are bold enough to obey Me and believe Me.

August 31

Psalms 42:8

Yet the Lord will command his lovingkindness in the daytime, and in the night his song shall be with me, and my prayer unto the God of my life.   KJV

When asked, you claim to be a sinner saved by grace. And so you are. But when asked, I claim you as a saint who's kept by the beauty of Christ. As you have structured your life under obedience to My Word, you have come to look more and more like this scripture. My lovingkindness -- yes it keeps you all the day -- because you have met with Me in prayer in the mornings. Before you rest in the night I hear you sing songs to Me, I hear you when you speak prayers and requests, but also praise to Me before you close your eyes and drift into sleep asking for Me to speak to you in your dreams. I am the God of your life. Stay close to Me. I sing over your rest. Your lifestyle is pleasing to Me, a sweet aroma. Child, you are Mine.

September 1

Isaiah 40:11

He shall feed his flock like a shepherd: he shall gather the lambs with his arm, and carry them in his bosom, and shall gently lead those that are with young. KJV

HE KNOWS MY NAME

Yes, I feed My flock. I carry the young. And those that are with young, they have a special spot in My heart as well. I lead them more gently. So much is changing in their bodies, their minds, their lives. As they prepare a room for their new little one, I prepare them to care for the child. I give moms extra wisdom. They will need it. Fathers as well, but moms even more so. They have the day to day nurturing, that will wear seemingly beyond their physical and mental limits. They have to know when danger exists to guard and protect. They need to nourish themselves as well as the child. Mothers need the instincts that are a characteristic of the shepherd. How often the heart cries of the mother -- is the one that moves Me the most. I listen for them in the night as she listens and is attune to her child's cry.

September 2

James 1:5-8

If any of you lack wisdom, let him ask of God, that giveth to all men liberally, and upbraideth not; and it shall be given him.

But let him ask in faith, nothing wavering. For he that wavereth is like a wave of the sea driven with the wind and tossed.

For let not that man think that he shall receive any thing of the Lord.

A double minded man is unstable in all his ways.   KJV

If you don't know what you're doing, pray to the Father. He loves to help. You'll get his help, and won't be condescended to when you ask for it. Ask boldly, believingly, without a second thought. People who "worry their prayers" are like wind-whipped waves. Don't think you're going to get anything from the Master that way, adrift at sea, keeping all your options open. The Message

Confidence is what I mean when I speak 'ask boldly'. So many come to Me and really just come to complain about how I handle things. You must come with petitions of course, I understand and even desire you to speak your wants and needs. But don't come whining because you don't like the way I do things. I am God after all. I do see things you don't. I do understand things you never will. It's like a child begging for the toy that was dropped on the rail road tracks, crying and screaming for it. However, you know full well a freight train is coming, and see they cannot have it that way. Trust Me enough to understand I have the big picture here, and your destiny is part of it, and so very precious to Me. Ask Me for wisdom in this. I want to give you that. If you're confused, come and meet with Me. Speak with Me. It's all about relationship. You will trust Me more and more, the more you meet with Me. Draw close. Don't wait for disaster to draw close. Have some wisdom, draw close to the Creator of all things, who loves and wants the best for you. Read the Psalms. Pick up My Word daily. Pray and praise and worship -- out loud! Dead religion prays only in their own little heads. I want you to speak to Me. Use your voice. I gave you that. Use your words. Words speak things into existence. This is Christian maturity 101. Rise up! I need your voice in this generation. Allow Me to use you to reach the lost.

September 3

Luke 24:47

And that repentance and remission of sins should be preached in his name among all nations, beginning at Jerusalem. KJV

He went on to open their understanding of the Word of God, showing them how to read their Bibles this way. He said, "You can see now how it is written that the Messiah suffers, rises from the dead on the third day, and then a total life-change through the

forgiveness of sins is proclaimed in his name to all nations --
starting from here, from Jerusalem! You're the first to hear and
see it. You're the witnesses. The Message

When My Son spoke these words, it was to His disciples - to open
their understanding of the Word of God. When you speak, many
times it is to open the understanding of the person you are speaking
to. Seeds of the Word of God are your responsibility in your
generation. As you plant the seed, I give the understanding. Even as
you are planting, you are receiving a deeper understanding as well.
My Word never ever returns void. That means, it hits home with the
listener. It also helps you as well. Don't underestimate the power of
the spoken word, especially when it is My Word. Use it today to
encourage someone. Your testimony of a changed life is important,
just make sure you let them know it was forgiveness of your sin
through the suffering, death and resurrection of Jesus that changed
your life. I'll open their understanding from there.

September 4

Titus 1:16

They profess that they know God; but in works they deny him,
being abominable, and disobedient, and unto every good work
reprobate. KJV

They say they know God, but their actions speak louder than their
words. They're real creeps, disobedient good-for-nothings.
The Message

People who know Me - do what I ask them to do. People claim all
kinds of things. Just because they say Lord, Lord, just because they
are able to write a catchy tune with a few of My scriptures contained

in it, does not make them a Christian, nor one of Mine. Disobedience corrupts the soul. Even their countenance will change, along with their actions of course. Their discernment will warp and their understanding will be shallow. Take care to obey My Word. Take care to do what I ask you to do, every day. If you are struggling with this, bring it to the cross. Lay it at My feet in morning prayer. I want to make you an overcomer in this, so that you will experience many victories in your walk.

September 5

Jeremiah 6:16-17

Thus saith the Lord, Stand ye in the ways, and see, and ask for the old paths, where is the good way, and walk therein, and ye shall find rest for your souls. But they said, We will not walk therein.

Also I set watchmen over you, saying, Hearken to the sound of the trumpet. But they said, We will not hearken. KJV

God's Message yet again: "Go stand at the crossroads and look around. Ask for directions to the old road, The tried-and-true road. Then take it. Discover the right route for your souls. But they said, 'It's a false alarm. It doesn't concern us.'   The Message

When you feel like you just keep witnessing and working with people and haven't seen much fruit, it is not always because you are not doing your part. Many times, it is merely the stubbornness of the ones I have asked you to work with. Remember it is all seed sown. Jeremiah had to work with a rebellious generation as well, and tell these folks some hard things. But he kept going, he just kept going. If you will do what I ask, I can change a nation. If you will do what I ask, I can change a generation. It will be one person at a time for you though. Look up, look around, as you go about your day. When I ask you to speak to someone, merely pull out a flier for your church or a gospel tract and pass it to them. If open, share your testimony of a changed life through the sacrifice of Jesus Christ. See what I do. One soul at a time. Don't be dissuaded by people who blow you off, or even tell you off. Do what I ask. Let Me take it from there. Take nothing personal, their frustrations are with Me, not you. Fellowship with co-laborers. This will help your spirit, and you will regain your confidence. Take one of them for coffee or dinner. You both need that. Walk the right roads, I will give you wisdom and strength.

September 6

Isaiah 41:13

For I the Lord thy God will hold thy right hand, saying unto thee, Fear not; I will help thee. KJV

Because I, your God, have a firm grip on you and I'm not letting go. I'm telling you, 'Don't panic. I'm right here to help you. The Message

When I speak it, it's a promise. You have nothing to fear, even in hard times. I always always have a firm grip on you. There's hope in the pain. Many times, joy and grief travel together. Out of the ashes, as the dust clears you will see Me. Even in the darkness of night, I am here, and if you look, you will see Me. Even when nothing else is visible. Look for Me. Speak to Me. I am here. When the rest of the world has seemed to abandoned you, I have not. I am always available to Mine. You are Mine. Set aside for kingdom purpose. Made to be anything but ordinary, you are designed for the extraordinary. Let Me build you. It will blow your mind who you will become. Come - meet with Me in prayer. That's where your strength begins this morning.

Isaiah 41:14-15

Fear not, thou worm Jacob, and ye men of Israel; I will help thee, saith the Lord, and thy redeemer, the Holy One of Israel.

Behold, I will make thee a new sharp threshing instrument having teeth: thou shalt thresh the mountains, and beat them small, and shalt make the hills as chaff.   KJV

"Do you feel like a lowly worm, Jacob? Don't be afraid. Feel like a fragile insect, Israel? I'll help you. I, God, want to reassure you. The God who buys you back, The Holy of Israel.

I'm transforming you from worm to harrow, from insect to iron. ..

verse 16 .. But you'll be confident and exuberant, expansive in The Holy of Israel!

The Message

Your enemies many times come in like a flood. As I shame them and confound them, they will become as nothing. However, I will make you iron in these processes. I will make you an instrument. You shall stand and the evil will fall away. Sometimes, in the good times, you forget there are enemies to fight. They have been driven away by Me, scattered. Rejoice in those times of peace. You will fight battles until you come home to be with Me. Keep that in mind. Peaceful times are times of refreshing. But stay close to Me. Do not wander. Stay strong. I've made you iron for a reason. There will be other battles. Stand firm. Find your confidence in Me, nowhere else. Keep your eyes open, especially your spiritual ones. This is the difference between maturity and lax.

September 8

James 3:5

*Even so the tongue is a little member, and boasteth great things.
Behold, how great a matter a little fire kindleth!   KJV*

*A word out of your mouth may seem of no account, but it can
accomplish nearly anything – or destroy it!   The Message*

You speak things as if it makes no difference to the person you are
speaking to. I have told you many times, be so careful as to what
comes out of your mouth. Jesus brought it up as well. In this
scripture My servant, James, is asking you to guard what you speak.
He is bringing a reminder to the church and early Christians in his
generation, but I had him write it in this letter to remind the
Christians of this generation, and you, of this very offense. It is
critical to guard the tongue. You win arguments. You have learned
to negotiate brilliantly. You coerce others into your way of thinking,
and that's not necessarily wrong, many times it's commendable.
You change hearts when you speak My Word. Also, be aware that
you have the ability with that same tongue to destroy hearts, dampen
spirits, ruin days and even lives with the harsh and critical words that
come out of that mouth of yours. How could you start and end
people's days with your venting and ugliness? It doesn't make you
feel any better either. It makes you feel ugly, because it is ugly.
Beauty truly is as beauty does. Keep your words full of beauty. I
know there are times for correction and hard things, I am not
speaking of those. I am speaking of your general conversation.
Love people. Love your family. Sometimes your kind word is the
only one they will receive today. Talk to others with the respect you
want others to show you. Do not ridicule. Mistakes happen.
Catastrophes happen. Help them process life correctly, then -- you

will process it correctly. Quit flying off the handle and expecting everyone else to allow that in their lives. You're bigger than that. Put your humble on. Meekness is strength under control. Show some control. You're Mine!

James 3:18 The fruit of righteousness is sown in peace of them that make peace. KJV

September 9

Luke 18:1-8

And he spake a parable unto them to this end, that men ought always to pray, and not to faint   KJV

Jesus told them a story showing that it was necessary for them to pray consistently and never quit. The Message

When Jesus spoke his stories, or parables, He spoke them to teach the people around Him, and the stories were recorded to teach you. Pay attention when you read His stories. If you don't understand what He is attempting to teach you, ask Me. I want to give you wisdom, and understanding. This particular story was told to teach you to pray consistently and to never ever quit. There are several reasons you must pray this way. First and foremost is because the enemy resists your prayers. You do have enemies in the spiritual realm. Remember Daniel persisted for 21 days. The widow in this parable was afflicted by her enemy. The ungodly judge that she went to see did not have any concern over her affliction, nor in the fact that she was a widow without a husband to protect her. He finally relented and gave her the vengeance, or justice, that she cried out for. The judge said, "Only because she keeps coming here and bothering me, I wanted her to go away." Her persistence paid off in deliverance from her enemy. The lesson Christ brought out of this was -- listen to what that unjust judge said. Her persistence pushed it through. Don't faint, don't quit, keep praying. Press through and fight your enemy. "Shall not God bring justice to His own?" was Jesus' reply. "He will, and he will speedily." But He related perseverance to faith. Do you have enough faith to pray it through? Take time and press in. The fervent prayer of a righteous saint does more in the spiritual realm than you understand. By faith, pray fervently, and out loud.

Luke 18:8

Nevertheless, when the Son of man cometh, shall he find faith on the earth?   KJV

September 10

Luke 11:1-4

One day he was praying in a certain place. When he finished, one of his disciples said, "Master, teach us to pray just as John taught his disciples." So he said, "When you pray, say,

Father, Reveal who you are

Set the world right.

Keep us alive with three square meals.

Keep us forgiven with you and forgiving others.

Keep us safe from ourselves and the Devil."   The Message

And it came to pass, that, as he was praying in a certain place, when he ceased, one of his disciples said unto him, Lord, teach us to pray, as John also taught his disciples.

And he said unto them, When ye pray, say,

Our Father which art in heaven, Hallowed be thy name.

Thy kingdom come. Thy will be done, as in heaven, so in earth.

Give us day by day our daily bread.

And forgive us our sins; for we also forgive every one that is indebted to us.

And lead us not into temptation; but deliver us from evil.   KJV

Prayer is most times simply a conversation with Me. It is you doing battle in the spiritual realm. Prayer was a major part of Jesus' life. He met with Me each morning at 4 am, and throughout His day, and just before every major event in His life on earth. Prayer is what sets men and women of God apart from the world. Your relationship with Me makes you unique. However, many struggles in your life are because you're not contending. This disciple of Christ's, that asked for help in his own prayer life, saw that John's disciples had something different operating in their prayer life. He wanted it. It wasn't a new convert asking for this direction, but a disciple, close to Him. You have My Holy Spirit indwelling in you, ask and I will teach you to pray. I want to guide you in this. You must have quality in your prayer. That's where the battle is won. A fervent Christian, and not just when there is a need, avails much. I am not a step-father, but close and intimate, you call Me -- Abba Father. You have that right. I love you beyond anything you understand. I am almighty, all powerful, but expect delays, be prepared. Delays do not mean 'no'. It takes maturity to wait. You are fighting a demonic force. Prayer speaks things in to life. Prayer gives Me the opportunity to create miracles and bring revival.

September 11

Galatians 5:22-23

But the fruit of the Spirit is love, joy, peace, longsuffering, gentleness, goodness, faith, meekness, temperance: against such there is no law.   KJV

But what happens when we live God's way? He brings gifts into our lives, much the same way that fruit appears in an orchard –

things like affection for others, exuberance about life, serenity.
We develop a willingness to stick with things, a sense of
compassion in the heart, and a conviction that a basic holiness
permeates things and people. We find ourselves involved in loyal
commitments, not needing to force our way in life, able to marshal
and direct our energies wisely. The Message

Are these fruits operating in your life? When you are frustrated that
the fruits are not evident in you, take time to draw closer to Me.
This is so that I can manifest Myself, My nature, in you. You will
never have these fruits without a close relationship with Me. Prayer
and reading the Word draws you close. So, when you pray for the
fruits, pray, "God? would you manifest yourself as patience in me
today?" "God? I need peace. Would you manifest yourself today in
me as peace?" I created you for this very thing. My fruits – My
nature – manifested through you – to accomplish great things. This
includes soul winning. When people see these fruits in you, My
nature evident in you, you will naturally draw them to you. They
will want to know why you have such peace, why you are able to be
loyal, why you are able to be patient in all seasons. I want you to
reach them for Me. Encouraging them that this life is available to
them as well, through repentance of sin, and the death and
resurrection of Jesus Christ. This is why He died. This is why He
rose again.

September 12

Luke 22:42
Saying, Father, if thou be willing, remove this cup from me:
nevertheless not my will, but thine, be done.   KJV

He pulled away from them about a stone's throw, knelt down, and
prayed, "Father, remove this cup from me. But please, not what I
want. What do you want?" At once an angel from heaven was at

his side strengthening him. He prayed on all the harder. Sweat, wrung from him like drops of blood, poured off his face.
The Message

Jesus knew the price of His obedience in this situation. He knew the sacrifice and the cost involved in His own personal pain on the cross. When I ask of you, do you just do what you want, when you want, with no thought of what I want? Somewhere you need to come to a place where you just do what is right, where you do what I've asked. At once the angels responded to Jesus' request for strength, read the scripture. You don't wait on angels anymore. My Spirit dwells in you for this purpose. Your strength comes from the Holy Spirit, immediately. Do you use that strength to enter farther and more fervently into the battles? Prayers before you drift off to sleep with a blanket over your head sound nice, and many times they will help your rest. However, that's not the battle I speak of here. Whispered prayers are lovely. However, that's not spiritual warfare at its best. Jesus prayed so fervently that He sweated drops of blood. What is your physical reaction when you contend in the spiritual. Or is there any? James' knees were so worn from contending that his friends lovingly called him 'camel knees'. Hannah's pastor was so amazed at her fervency at the altar that he thought she had been drinking. Jesus pulled away, knelt down, and got into prayer. Do you?

James 4:10 Get down on your knees before the Master; it's the only way you'll get on your feet. The Message

September 13

Psalms 96:5-6

God made the heavens –

Royal splendor radiates from him,

A powerful beauty sets him apart. The Message

For all the gods of the nations are idols; but the Lord made the heavens.

Honour and majesty are before him: strength and beauty are in his sanctuary.   *KJV*

Praise and worship changes things. When you don't understand exactly how, open the psalms. David moved My heart, and also My hand on many occasions with simple praise and worship. He understood the spiritual dynamics of this. This pulls down strongholds the enemy has built between us. This ushers in My presence and brings restoration to your soul and to your faith. When you don't know how, simply read the psalms out loud. The spoken word is powerful. Get to know Me. The psalms are full of My character and nature, purely so that you are able to draw near to Me.

September 14

Proverbs 14:1
Every wise woman buildeth her house;
but the foolish plucketh it down with her hands.   *KJV*

Lady Wisdom builds a lovely home;
Sir Fool comes along and tears it down brick by brick.
The Message

Many a woman has destroyed her home in anger and frustration. Wisdom should always overcome raw emotions. If you will pray for wisdom, the wisdom that comes from Me, this will be what changes your control over your emotions. Many a day they run wild because of lack of wisdom. Wisdom builds a network of habits that make the simple things run and work throughout your day. Without these habits, confusion will ensue. Usually it will come in the form of lost time, lost confidence in yourself, or lost confidence in others. Then – whoops – here comes confusion. The devil is a master at igniting a woman's emotions in the time of chaos. If you would but remember to look up to Me and take time in the midst of chaos to ask Me for help, I will help. Start your mornings with prayer, no matter what distraction comes your way. If you will come near to Me in the mornings, I will make a straight path in your day and ease your load. This will give you insight to build, rather than pulling your home down in error. You will rest at the end of your day in a lovely home, and so will those who share it. I want to give you that, I also want to give your family that.

September 15

Proverbs 14:2

An honest life shows respect for God;

A degenerate life is a slap in his face.   *The Message*

He that walketh in his uprightness feareth the Lord;

but he that is perverse in his ways despiseth him.   *KJV*

When you display to the world a respect and honor for Me, you turn heads. Never underestimate the power of your testimony of a changed life through Jesus Christ. Do your best to keep your testimony amongst others. Degenerates, those who ignore My Word, especially those that call themselves Christians, bring dishonor to Me. You have struggles, you have challenges, bring them to Me, so that I can help you be victorious over them. Obey Me, trust Me, and watch how I move in your life. And the ones who turned their heads in the first place? They will see as well. Be the overcomer. That brings Me glory. That brings Me joy. That brings you joy as well.

Proverbs 27:12

A prudent man sees evil and hides himself and avoids it,

But the naïve [who are easily misled] continue on and are
punished [by suffering the consequences of sin].   AMP

A prudent person sees trouble coming and ducks;
a simpleton walks in blindly and is clobbered.   The Message

A prudent man foreseeth the evil, and hideth himself;
but the simple pass on, and are punished.   KJV

Solomon is making a case for Me here. There is much evil in your
generation as well. There should have been and could have been
warnings made, out loud, but red lights and warnings were ignored
at many situations in your generation. Three huge examples, the
landing of Katrina, the catastrophe of Chernobyl, and yes, even
9/11. Some simple disciplines were avoided which caused many to
lose their lives. Do you ignore warning signs and red lights and bells
and whistles in your life? I gave you a mind that could see ahead.
This is called foreseeing. It means to take a careful look, have some
awareness of your situation, perceive what is coming, ponder things,
figure things out, plan ahead. Jesus told you, watch and pray. I gave
you this long-range vision so that you could avoid the trouble ahead.
Stay on the cutting edge of prayer. Stay involved with wise counsel.
You have many resources in Me, take time to ask for them. But
don't ignore them. Namaan almost missed a healing because of
ignoring his counsel. He had no idea where that miracle would
come from because of a pride issue. It is said, look before you leap.
Slow down, think! My yoke truly is easy. My burdens truly are light.
Give Me yours. If you will watch and pray, as your greatest

Counselor told you, then obey, you will find the greatest peace you've ever known.

September 17

2 Cor 6:1-10

But in all things approving ourselves as the ministers of God
KJV

Companions as we are in this work with you, we beg you, please
don't squander one bit of this marvelous life God has given us.
God reminds us, I heard your call in the nick of time; The day you
needed me, I was there to help. Well, now is the right time to
listen, the day to be helped. Don't put it off; don't frustrate God's
work by showing up late, throwing a question mark over
everything we're doing. Our work as God's servants gets validated
– or not – in the details. People are watching us as we stay at our
post, alertly, unswervingly …
In hard times, tough times, bad times; when we're beaten up,
jailed, and mobbed; working hard, working late, working without
eating; with pure heart, clear head, steady hand; in gentleness,
holiness, and honest love; when we're telling the truth, and when
God's showing his power; when we're doing our best setting things
right; when we're praised, and when we're blamed; slandered, and
honored; true to our word, though distrusted; ignored by the
world, but recognized by God; terrifically alive, though rumored to
be dead; beaten within an inch of our lives, but refusing to die;
immersed in tears, yet always filled with deep joy; living on
handouts, yet enriching many; having nothing, having it all.
The Message

As evident by Paul's writings, you are not the only one to go through trials as a Christian. Try to remember this when in the thick of things. Bring praise and worship to carry you through. Paul sang in his cell, he worshipped through his trials. This is why he could write such things. You will go through things, just because you are Mine. You will face difficulties, just because you are Mine. I am building and strengthening you for eternity. Always remember I am right there with you. You don't just wear the team t-shirt as some do, you are filled with My Holy Spirit. Look to Me. I will carry you, no matter what. Do your best to remember to pray. When you have done all you can to stand, just stand. Your ministry is souls saved, the lost restored, go ye, taking it to the streets, to be about your Father's business, contending for your generation, rising up, turning the page, co-laboring with Me. Your contentment is with where I have put you. When you realize you are in My will, you're able to carry on in a settled-ness. Sell out for the gospel, find the joy of salvation and share it, sacrifice all the worldliness, be willing to put the kingdom before all other things. It's only stuff that will burn. My will and your victories can never be taken away from you. Every witness, every testimony of yours spoken, will live forever. Does that motivate you? Your life blood is the one on one witness to others. To share My Word with the lost soul. Jesus set your example. Paul ran with that example. He knew if he was right with Me, the rest didn't matter. What he had or didn't. There is a revelation here for you. Nothing is more important than your laboring for the Kingdom. Be one-eyed. Make every conflict in your life be over the gospel, over souls, live it, wherever you go. The 'I'll do it later" attitude is a road to disaster. The souls are crying out for you. The issue is they're going to hell. You don't have all the time in the world as you think you do. Do not let 'things' come between you and the harvest.

September 18

Psalms 18:28

For thou wilt light my candle: the Lord my God will enlighten my darkness.   KJV

In the darkness of trials, because they do seem very dark sometimes, I will bring the light. Look past them, and see Me. Look around them, and see Me. Hide yourself in My shadow. I will place a wing about you and carry you through them. I am your light. I am the light of the world. When I say that, it is because it is true. The light of the sun outside goes down at the end of the day. When the storms come, the clouds gather, the darkness and the dimness ensue. My light never goes out. The darkness is the enemy's distraction from Me. Look past it. I am here.

September 19

Matthew 6:30-34

Wherefore, if God so clothe the grass of the field, which to day is, and to morrow is cast into the oven, shall he not much more clothe you, O ye of little faith?

Therefore take no thought, saying, What shall we eat? or, What shall we drink? or, Wherewithal shall we be clothed?

(For after all these things do the Gentiles seek:) for your heavenly Father knoweth that ye have need of these things.

But seek ye first the kingdom of God, and his righteousness; and all these things shall be added unto you.

Take therefore no thought for the morrow: for the morrow shall take thought for the things of itself. Sufficient unto the day is the evil thereof. KJV

"If God gives such attention to the appearance of wildflowers – most of which are never even seen – don't you think he'll attend to you, take pride in you, do his best for you?

What I'm trying to do here is to get you to relax, to not be so preoccupied with getting, so you can respond to God's giving. People who don't know God and the way he works fuss over these things, but you know both God and how he works.

Steep your life in God-reality, God-initiative, God-provisions.
Don't worry about missing out. You'll find all your everyday
human concerns will be met." The Message

The things people leave Me for are the very things I promise to
provide. As you collect and strategize for more, do you see it
becomes a stagnant flow? When you are in want of anything, look
around, give something away. When you give, not sell, give, I can
bless that. When you hoard and keep, it stops the flow through.
Think of it like this, both hands open. One hand receives and the
other is open to give. When the giving hand closes, so does the
receiving hand. I cannot give, when you stop the flow through.
When you open your giving hand, Mine is able to accommodate as
well. Some say, 'Don't give just to receive.' I say, "Give, and
watch what I do, watch My response." It's a kingdom principle that
will begin to operate in your life. Your priorities will change. What
seems important today really isn't tomorrow. As you enter into this
arena you will truly see, it really is better to give than to receive. It's
a joy you won't experience any other way.

September 20

Romans 1:23
And changed the glory of the uncorruptible God into an image
made like to corruptible man, and to birds, and fourfooted beasts,
and creeping things. KJV

They traded the glory of God who holds the whole world in his
hands for cheap figurines you can buy at any roadside stand.
The Message

When any religion teaches you to bow in a certain direction, or light
candles, or reverence any statue, run for your life. That is not Me.
That is an idol. I want relationship with you. You cannot have
relationship with a piece of wood or plastic trinket hanging on your

mirror. I am your Creator, and yes, I hold the whole world in My hands, not yours. People who form idols also form their new god's ideology and rules. In other words, they form their own god, inside and out. Then they sit back and expect it to bless them. Ridiculous. I am sovereign. If you want to draw near to Me, come in humility and respect and most of all repentance. I want to change your life, but it won't be on your terms, it will be on Mine. Walk in the newness of Christ, as you surrender to Him, and your life will never be the same again. Look back in six months and you won't even recognize yourself. Idolatry is sin and death and only leads to destruction. Jesus Christ truly is life and life more abundantly.

September 21

Romans 1: 21, 25
Because that, when they knew God, they glorified him not as God, neither were thankful; ...

Who changed the truth of God into a lie, and worshipped and served the creature more than the Creator, who is blessed for ever. Amen   KJV

What happened was this: People knew God perfectly well, but when they didn't treat him like God, refusing to worship him, ...

..they traded the true God for a fake god, and worshiped the god they made instead of the God who made them – the God we bless, the God who blesses us. Oh, yes!   The Message

When you come to know Me, I fill a void in the heart that is there to be filled, specifically by Me. When you refuse to glorify Me, and are not even thankful, a hardness comes to the heart. You try so desperately to fill that void and emptiness with something else. More of this stuff, and more of that stuff, even addictions come flooding in. This is where the fake gods enter in. Because that void can't be filled without Me, you attempt to fill it with something else.

Pride fights as your flesh rises up – all against your relationship with Me. The counterfeits pop up their ugly heads as hell lays out a strategy for your soul through idol worship. Paul was speaking of his generation in this text; however, your generation professes wisdom and has become fools as well. Take a look around you. Pay close attention to how they love to hear the lie, rather than truth. It is so easy to get caught up in this when you take the Creator of heaven and earth off the throne of your heart and replace him with the trinkets and trimmings of this world. Not only is this an abomination to Me, but it is also an abomination to yourself. You sell yourself short and end up destroyed at the end of the day. Idol worship is dangerous territory. People are sick and diseased and mentally ill, because they have opened up the door to this practice. When they open this door; they allow hell access to them. To close this door – you must repent – surrender your life to Christ – and change your behavior through the blood of the cross – and display your thankfulness for your salvation by glorifying My Name, every day. There is only one name under heaven, given amongst men, whereby you can be saved. Christ is truth. Christ is victorious. Christ is the way. Christ is the life. No man comes to the Father, but through Him.

September 22

Psalms 18:19
He brought me forth also into a large place; he delivered me, because he delighted in me.   KJV

...God stuck by me. He stood me up on a wide-open field; I stood there saved -- surprised to be loved!   The Message

When you are caught in the midst of the enemy's chaos and hate: I am always reaching down and bringing the way out. Sometimes I'll simply show you a word to carry you through. Other times I'll remove you. Other times I'll remove the storm. But I am always right there in the midst with you. When I say I will stand closer than a brother, I absolutely mean it. Look up, your redemption draws nigh. Hope will be realized. You are loved beyond your wildest imagination- you are loved by Me, your Creator, your Savior. On the other side of this storm, like David, you will stand in awe. And you will stand, stronger than ever!

Proverbs 16:18
First pride, then the crash -- the bigger the ego, the harder the fall.
The Message

Pride blinds you. It makes it so that you can't even see how you are affecting others. Your sharp tongue gets in the way of fruitfulness. Who wants to be around that? Your demanding that everyone else live like you do, cripples your effectiveness in My kingdom. Bringing Me glory, is not bragging about your accomplishments. Although you will have many accomplishments when you live for Me. Don't do things so you get the glory, do them so that I do. This will release you from the grip of the spirit of pride on your life. If you think you are humble, that would be your first clue that you are not. Repent, follow Me. I can help you with this. Guard your tongue and think before you speak. Will God get any glory from what I am about to say? Love others just for love's sake. This breaks the back of pride. You'll fight pride until you come to heaven. However, you must actively fight it. It's a huge pesky spiritual obstacle to My will in your life and those that you affect around you. If you allow pride to build up in your life, you will crash and burn. It's a spiritual truth. Humbleness will truly usher out pride and only then will there be room for joy and peace.

September 24

1 Timothy 3:1,2,6
This is a true saying, If a man desire the office of a bishop, he desire to a good work.
A bishop must be ...
Not a novice, lest being lifted up with pride he fall into the condemnation of the devil.   KJV

If anyone wants to provide leadership in the church, good!
But there are preconditions:
He must not be a new believer, lest the position go to his head and the devil trip him up.   The Message

You must take a breath each day, and realize - this is a spiritual warfare - a true battle you will fight today. You are designed for a purpose. Leadership is for the seasoned Christian. The daily battles are to build you for exactly this - leadership. Your life's battles will cause the impurities in you to rise to the surface so they can be dealt with. This is a kingdom process. The thing that will ooze out in abundance is pride. Pride does come before the fall. Pride must be dealt with. There will be no personal growth, nor fruit, when pride stands in the way. Pride is contagious and spreads like a disease. The end of pride is destruction because you will come to a place where you cannot even admit to Me that you are wrong, let alone anyone else. This is dangerous considering Jesus reminded you to repent daily. Pride left unchecked, unrepented, breeds contempt. Have any contempt or ill feelings towards anyone today? Do you see everybody else's faults when sitting and thinking at the end of your day? That is pride manifesting its ugly head to trip you up. Bring it with a humble and repented heart to the altar. I can help you process these things correctly.

September 25

1 John 2:16
For all that is in the world, the lust of the flesh, and the lust of the eyes, and the pride of life, is not of the Father, but is of the world. And the world passeth away, and the lust thereof: but he that doeth the will of God abideth for ever. **KJV**

The pride of life - wanting to look good or appear important - is not of Me. I'm not saying you can't look decent and carry yourself well. I am saying there is a line that gets crossed that shouldn't be. Pride is a huge spiritual stumbling block. Pride is an entity that you will fight continually. When it rears its ugly head in your life it is hard to see around it. You're so worried about self - you simply cannot be bothered with anyone else. You think of 'their' misery as their own doing. "Why would it be my affair?" you ask yourself. When you get confused if you should help them or not - take a quick inventory of the influences at work in your heart in the spiritual realm right now. Ask Me, I'll reveal them. You don't hand a drug addict $20 for diapers when you know full well it's really going for another high.

But how about that gal who really is struggling? I don't bless you so you can hoard it. I bless you for a flow-through: to the poor, the down trodden, the empty hearted and the sick. When you kick pride to the curb you will enter in to a spiritual truth and totally different way of looking at people and yourself. Don't be so caught up in 'you' today. Give it a rest. Look around. Give something away. This will help you break that prideful, selfishness in you today.

September 26

Proverbs 6:17
These six things doth the Lord hate: yea, seven are an abomination unto him:
A proud look,
a lying tongue, and
hands that shed innocent blood.
An heart that deviseth wicked imaginations,
feet that be swift in running to mischief.
A false witness that speaketh lies,
and he that soweth discord among the brethren.   KJV

Here are six things God hates, and one more that he loathes with a passion:
eyes that are arrogant,
a tongue that lies,
hands that murder the innocent,
a heart that hatches evil plots,
feet that race down a wicked track,
a mouth that lies under oath,
a troublemaker in the family.   The Message

Pride. It irks Me. The reason it irks Me of course is the sin involved. Also, it irks Me because of the destruction it causes so many in the way of it. Not only will unchecked pride kill you - it will kill all those you have influence over. Why? Because it spreads like a wildfire. It will breed and seed into all you touch. Notice Solomon put it at the top of the list? He watched it breed into his men and manifest itself into all of the rest of this list. Pride will take you places you never intended on going. You will wake up one day and not even know how your life and circumstances got so out of hand. Jesus said, 'Repent every morning.' This breaks the back of pride. Daily humility before the throne brings more victory over pride than anything else. Take time for morning prayer. This is a fight that must be fought. Take time to remove self from the throne of your life and replace it with Me.

September 27

James 4:6
But he giveth more grace. Wherefore he saith, God resisteth the proud, but giveth grace unto the humble. KJV

And what he gives in love is far better than anything else you'll find. It's common knowledge that "God goes against the willful proud; God gives grace to the willing humble." The Message

Pride manifests in so many different forms in your life. Even when it pokes its head out to make you see it in others. You know that thought, "Geesh, they're awfully prideful." Look at the two interpretations of this scripture. 'I give more grace' and 'I give more love'. They ride hand in hand. It is impossible to love someone and not extend grace. It is impossible to extend grace without some sort of love in your heart. Love doesn't exploit faults in others. When you see faults or they are magnified, it is probably hell manifesting to point them out. Not everybody, but most people are just living life, not necessarily out to make your day miserable. A servant goes through many challenges. This will be one of them. Look past their faults, and be humble enough not to speak of their errors, and to chase the thought of their shortcomings away. Love them instead. It will help you resist pride. Lovely is as lovely does. Grace is given as grace is given.

September 28

1 Peter 5:5
Likewise, ye younger, submit yourselves unto the elder. Yea, all of you be subject one to another, and be clothed with humility: for God resisteth the proud, and giveth grace to the humble. KJV

And you who are younger must follow your leaders. But all of you, leaders and followers alike, are to be down to earth with each other, for --
  God has had it with the proud, But takes delight in just plain people.   The Message

People from the beginning of time have been just like you. The old-time bible stories are stories of ordinary folks, who like you, live ordinary lives. The ones who stand out in My book and do extraordinary things -by My standards- are those that tapped into My will. I can generally use plain people who desire Me to use them. It is very difficult to use the proud. They won't take time to listen to Me, nor obey Me when they do happen to hear My voice. Pride keeps them from instruction. Pride knows everything and insists their way is best - not even their God can make a better decision than them. If your mindset seems to be - 'who do they think they are to correct me?' - or - 'that'll never work' - when you haven't even listened to the idea - you are selling yourself short actually. You dwarf yourself and your own growth without learning from each other. Clothe yourself with humility. That means back off and let the other one speak. There are 100 ways to accomplish this task. They all might work. But I want you to find the will of your God in this. That's where you'll grow. Slow down and listen. Ask Me to help, I will. Remember meekness? Meekness is strength under control. Bind pride. Embrace humility. This will change everything.

September 29

Proverb 29:1
He, that being often reproved hardeneth his neck, shall suddenly be destroyed, and that without remedy.   KJV

For people who hate discipline and only get more stubborn, There'll come a day when life tumbles in and they break, but by then it'll be too late to help them.   The Message

Have you ever met a child who is seldom corrected? That spirit is alive and well in planet earth today. Just like it was when I had Paul pen this. Stubbornness is a fruit of pride. When you are disciplined or corrected - check your spirit. This will give you clear evidence of the power that pride has in your character. Repent of pride. Fight it. This is your enemy. This will destroy you. Do not allow pride to rule your life. You must have the upper hand in this spiritual warfare that you fight. Pride is a key enemy. Check your armor.

Ephesians 6:14-18
Stand therefore, having your loins girt about with truth, and having on the breastplate of righteousness;
And your feet shod with the preparation of the gospel of peace;
Above all, taking the shield of faith, wherewith ye shall be able to quench all the fiery darts of the wicked.
And take the helmet of salvation, and the sword of the Spirit, which is the word of God:
Praying always...in the Spirit...for the saints.   KJV

September 30

Proverbs 29:25
The fear of man bringeth a snare: but whoso putteth his trust in the Lord shall be safe.   KJV

The fear of human opinion disables; trusting in God protects you from that.   The Message

When you trust Me with what to speak, you will no longer fear what they think. Bring circumstances to Me in morning prayer. Talk to Me about it. Let Me fill you with My Spirit today so that you can have that confidence in the spoken word. Slow down and speak what I tell you. Have a humbleness in the way you handle people. Things are not always what they seem to be, so get the whole picture before you speak. That means listen, ask questions, then form an opinion and voice it by what My Word says. I'll bring it to you. I'll bring them to you. I'll use you to change a generation, one person, one situation at a time.

OCTOBER

October 1

Hebrews 12:3
For consider him that endured such contradiction of sinners
against himself, lest ye be wearied and faint in your minds. KJV

When you find yourselves flagging in your faith, go over that story
again, item by item, that long litany of hostility he plowed through.
That will shoot adrenaline into your souls!   The Message

HE KNOWS MY NAME

Weariness will come. Rest must be taken at times. I make you lie down in green pastures. There's a reason for this. I request your presence in prayer and fellowship with Me. There's a reason. I carry your burden. There's a reason. I have purpose and destiny for you. These are linked with Me and are linked with My will. Jesus taught you to pray - 'Father, your will be done on earth as it is in heaven.' Align your life with Christ. Read the 4 gospels. Learn His prayer habits, His humility, His boldness, His strengths, His ways with people, His patience to go completely out of His way - to do My will. Rest in Jesus. Rest in the Word. It is strength for your soul. Eyes forward - think of heaven.

Hebrews 12:2
Looking unto Jesus the author and finisher of our faith; who for the joy that was set before him endured the cross, despising the shame, and is set down at the right hand of the throne of God. KJV

Keep your eyes on Jesus, who both began and finished this race we're in. Study how he did it. Because he never lost sight of where he was headed--that exhilarating finish in and with God--he could put up with anything along the way: Cross, shame, whatever. And now he's there, in the place of honor, right alongside God.
The Message

October 2

1 Peter 5:4
And when the chief Shepherd shall appear, ye shall receive a crown of glory that fadeth not away. KJV

When I come in open rule you will be commended and that will never fade away. Press on towards the high calling. When it seems, you can't go on today, just place one foot in front of the other. Your rewards and crowns in eternity will far surpass anything on this earth. Your mind cannot comprehend, simply because your eyes have never seen, nor your brain ever imagined, the things that await you on this side of heaven. Keep your eyes towards Me. Trust Me. I keep My promises. Eternity is forever.

Isaiah 28:5
In that day shall the Lord of hosts be for a crown of glory, and for a diadem of beauty, unto the residue of his people.   KJV

The prophet is speaking of a day to come. When your Savior, Jesus, My Son, came on the scene - time shifted. A dispensation of grace and salvation through the light of Christ, established by His death and resurrection, began. When His second coming commences - eternity will be ushered in. Many events, some foretold, will take place between then and now. The issue today, however, is your soul. Will you accept the grace of God, and salvation offered by the sacrifice of the Lamb? Jesus died for a reason. It was for you. As you bow your knee and surrender all of heaven takes notice, but especially Me. I will be your beauty. You will receive the crown of glory. The prophet refers to a 'diadem' - or tiara - that will be the beauty. You cannot serve Me and not end up anything but beautiful. Follow Me, obey Me. In six months turn around and look at your life. The beauty will astound you.

Isaiah 62:3,5
Thou shalt also be a crown of glory in the hand of the Lord, and a royal diadem in the hand of thy God.
... So shall thy God rejoice over thee.   KJV

2 Timothy 4:7-8
I have fought a good fight, I have finished my course, I have kept the faith;
Henceforth there is laid up for me a crown of righteousness, which the Lord, the righteous judge, shall give me at that day: and not to me only, but unto all them also that love his appearing. KJV

I have commanded you to fight. I have commanded you to run the race. I have commanded you to keep a faith in Me. My promises are true. Your crown of righteousness will be realized on that day as with many other rewards. My people are a peculiar people. They don't run after the things of the world, nor the things that the people of the world think they should. They stand out in a crowd. Many times, ridiculed by this world, but stand out nonetheless. When they seek Me, I'm found. When they ask Me, I answer. A relationship is two ways. I hear you. My people take time to hear Me.

October 5

Zechariah 9:16
And the Lord their God shall save them in that day as the flock of his people: for they shall be as the stones of a crown, lifted up as an ensign upon his land.   KJV

Their God will save the day. He'll rescue them. They'll become like sheep, gentle and soft. Or like gemstones in a crown, catching all the colors of the sun. Then how they'll shine! shimmer! glow! the young men robust! the young women lovely!   The Message

My people are precious to Me. After that day, the war of wars, I will lift them up and they shall be like a flag - a banner - lifted up across the land. A victory won such as has never been won in all of time. As I mold and shape you today, keep your head up, eyes forward and think of these things. As a precious and costly jewel in My crown - please remember Me - please remember I will never leave you nor forsake you. Let Me direct your footsteps. Let Me carry your burdens. I have a ton of purpose for you. Trust Me. I want to make sure you make it - filled with glory!

October 6

Revelation 3:11-12
Behold, I come quickly: hold that fast which thou hast, that no man take thy crown.
Him that overcometh will I make a pillar in the temple of my God ..
KJV

"I'm on my way; I'll be there soon. Keep a tight grip on what you have so no one distracts you and steals your crown."
"I'll make each conqueror a pillar in the sanctuary of my God, a permanent position of honor ... "   The Message

I will be there sooner than it seems now. I am preparing an awesome place for you. Be patient. Be vigilant. Be diligent. When I return I will be returning for those that are about My Father's business. If you love Me - you obey His Word. I left each of you with a task and a purpose. If you are not clear on which task or which purpose - come to Me and ask again. I don't mind showing you. How could I expect you to perform a task unless I showed you and instructed you? Carry on - process life well - eternity in heaven is just a hands breadth away.

October 7

Matthew 19:3
The Pharisees also came unto him, tempting him, and saying unto him, ...   KJV

Your greatest enemies come with words. They will speak words and begin to pressure you into speaking words back that undermine your ministry, your family and even your life. They speak words of sickness. They speak words of perversion. They speak words of gossip and slander. They speak to you just to trip you up into justifying their own sins. They speak words to destroy you. In this scenario the interpretation from the Greek came out as 'tempting him'. And they were. However, there's more to it. You must look at the entire picture here. These men, educated in the law and schooled in the thoughts of the land, knew full well the answers to their questions. They were trying him, testing him, asking questions just to provoke him, badgering him even. Note how He answered. He answered with the Word of God, that came through Moses. They respected Moses. Jesus brilliantly exposed truth on a level they could understand, even though truth was not what they were seeking. When they come at you - if you can learn to assess the situation and use My Word - scripture - as your weapon of choice - you can impart things in them that will never return void. Look past what they're saying - and see Me. Of course, listen, you need to answer them with respect and a heart for people, but remember the enemy is after you. And the enemy is after them. Use My Word whenever possible. Speak it out loud into people's lives. You don't need to cite chapter and verse but you do need to look and see the true need and speak life and life more abundantly into the people that cross your path.

Jeremiah 33:2-3
Thus saith the Lord the maker thereof, the Lord that formed it, to establish it; the Lord is his name;
Call unto me, and I will answer thee, and shew thee great and mighty things, which thou knowest not.   KJV

This is God's Message, the God who made earth, made it livable and lasting, known everywhere as GOD:
'Call to me and I will answer you. I'll tell you marvelous and wondrous things that you could never figure out on your own.'
The Message

Call - I want to show you things, things you don't already know. Be teachable - open to Me - to My Word - to correction. I want to make you wise. I want to give understanding to you to further My purposes. I want to show you how I want you to be used in the kingdom. Never speak - "I know I'm not good enough for that!" Always speak, "I will need God's help to accomplish this." This will change the dynamics of any situation. You will also affect the ones around you who see the dynamics of faith displayed and practiced. This is truly a gift of the Spirit. I want you involved in those gifts. Call - this gives Me opportunity to speak and act.

1 Corinthians 15:33
But don't fool yourselves. Don't let yourselves be poisoned by this anti-resurrection loose talk. "Bad company ruins good manners".
The Message

Be careful who you hang with. It's good to witness to people. It's great to love and bless people. But be very careful where you hang your hat, and who hangs their hat at your house. Fellowship is critical. It changes lives. So new converts must be involved with the older saints to have instruction on how to live life for Christ. Exampleship is always the best way. But people who have no interest in the gospel are corrupt and in turn corrupt those they come in contact with. And most of the time it is on purpose. Many delight in the destruction and corruption of a saint of Mine. Use common sense, use wisdom, don't be fooled. When they expose themselves with anti-Christ rhetoric, literally pick up your head and look and listen. Never leave yourselves vulnerable to these. Do not enter into partnerships or debt with them. Keep the upper hand and a way of escape. Don't invite them back into your home, and find a way to usher them out. Witness, share the gospel, but when there is no repentance, be cautious.

October 10

Luke 9:1-5
Jesus now called the Twelve and gave them authority and power to deal with all the demons and cure diseases. He commissioned them to preach the news of God's kingdom and heal the sick. He said, "Don't load yourselves up with equipment. Keep it simple; you are the equipment. And no luxury inns -- get a modest place and be content there until you leave. If you're not welcomed, leave town. Don't make a scene. Shrug your shoulders and move on."
The Message

You are spiritually equipped. I would not have called you to this, and then left you unequipped or set up to fail. I've equipped you to succeed, that's where I get the glory, in the victory. You are more than enough. You see the spiritual enemy. You have authority as a blood bought believer. You operate from a position of strength, not weakness. I spoke you into existence. It is not what it looks like, and you know this from your spiritual perspective. The truth you stand on defeats the lies. You are full of My Word and this defeats the enemy. My grace stands you far above the circumstances. You believe it, and make right decisions because of that faith. You wear right living on your chest. Your spoken words are released into the spiritual realm and defeat hell. You use My Word effectively. You have learned to stand in victory.

October 11

Proverbs 11:2
When pride cometh, then cometh shame: but with the lowly is wisdom. KJV
The stuck-up fall flat on their faces, but down-to-earth people stand firm. The Message

Pride comes in many shapes and sizes. Look around. You can see it ever so clearly in everybody else. But in you! Pride seems to keep its fingers in your ears, and its hands over your eyes. You are deaf and blind to its manifestations in your own life and being. It's time to root out pride. It's time to heat it up like dross in silver - scrape it off the top - and heat it up some more - because it is stubborn and hangs on tight. Why is pride so hard for the human to overcome? Because the spirit of pride is so well masked in the love of self. Self on the throne is the number one goal of hell. With this as an anchor, so much more can creep through that open door into your life. You must overcome pride with spiritual warfare. This has got to begin with morning prayer. A humbling of yourself before the throne of your God will change the dynamics of your day. Stay prayed up. This gives you the high ground in any battle you will face. Don't forget the armor. Paul spelled it out for you in Ephesians chapter 6. Learn it, memorize it! Be a mighty warrior. Mighty warriors seek the high ground and never leave the armor forgotten when they enter the battle. And don't forget to be able to take some direction and correction in life. If your commander can't tell you which way to go on the battlefield, and by the way your sword needs sharpening, then you'll end up dead. You got this, when you take it seriously.

October 12

Romans 8:37
Nay, in all these things we are more than conquerors through him
that loved us. KJV

There is nothing on this earth you cannot accomplish. Do you know why? I'll tell you why. Because you are Mine. I indwell in you. My Holy Spirit finishes you. Completes you. Tap into that reality. You cannot humanly understand it. It must come by faith and revelation. But it is true nonetheless. I am involved in everything in your life, since the day you surrendered to Me. Trust Me. I can carry you, ignite you, help you process life, so that you are the best you can be. More than a conqueror. You don't just conquer. More than victorious. You don't just win. You are Mine!

Philippians 4:1
Therefore, my brethren dearly beloved and longed for, my joy and
crown, so stand fast in the Lord, my dearly beloved. KJV
My dear, dear friends! I love you so much. I do want the very best
for you. You make me feel such joy, fill me with such pride. Don't
waver. Stay on track, steady in God. The Message

Look about you. The devil speaks to you many times, 'you have no
friends.' Even you, yourself say, 'I need a friend.' I say, 'You have
many more than you realize.' These are your friends. Your church.
Your work. Your neighbors. Be a good friend and love them just as
they are. If they don't know Me, share Me when you can. But always
try your best to be a friend. I've placed you right where I want you,
geographically and historically. This is your world. These are your
contemporaries. Love them. They need it. I can help you with that.
Give and it shall be given back to you. Love people.

1 Thessalonians 2:19-20
For what is our hope, or joy, or crown of rejoicing? Are not even
ye in the presence of our Lord Jesus Christ at his coming?
For ye are our glory and joy. KJV

Who do you think we're going to be proud of when our Master
Jesus appears if it's not you?
You're our pride and joy! The Message

Fruitfulness is a rewarding experience. Take time with people. You
can't win them if you won't take time with them. They won't change
without an influence of godly lives. I know you're busy today. Don't
fill up your life with so much 'to do's' that encouraging someone
won't fit into your day. You have got to answer phones when they
call. It's called communication. You have got to visit the sick. It's
called encouragement. You have got to visit the elderly. They are
lonely. The bereaved need a sound voice in their ear today to pick up
their spirit. Do for each other. Do for a sinner too. Show them Me,
through your kindnesses.

Revelation 4:4,6,10
And round about the throne were four and twenty seats: and upon
the seats I saw four and twenty elders sitting, clothed in white
raiment; and they had on their heads crowns of gold.

And before the throne there was a sea of glass like unto crystal...

The four and twenty elders fall down before him that sat on the
throne, and worship him that liveth for ever and ever, and cast
their crowns before the throne...   KJV

When someone wants to tell you heaven does not exist - take a stroll
through the book of Revelation. I showed that glimpse to John so
that he would record it for you. I showed that to John to encourage
him in his life of trials. I show that glimpse to you for the same
purpose. Without a hope - people perish. Without a hope - they have
no purpose. Share that hope with someone today. If they have no
hope - what do they have to live for? What do they have to die for?
Take time to share My hope today. Watch a life change. It's an
amazing and inspiring thing to be a part of. Be about your Father's
business. It's what you were created to do. It's good for your soul.

October 16

Psalms 132:18
His enemies will I clothe with shame: but upon himself shall his
crown flourish. KJV
I'll dress his enemies in dirty rags, but I'll make his crown sparkle
with splendor. The Message

You have many enemies amongst you. Sometimes you recognize
them, most times you don't. But I know them. I have a view of the
heart that you do not. I see their motives. I see the things they
themselves wouldn't think of posting on social media for all the
world to see. Count on this, I have your back. I'll turn things around
for all of it to work together for good for those that love Me and are
called according to My purpose. Don't be deceived. I got this. You
want to end up sparkling? Follow Me.

HE KNOWS MY NAME

October 17

1 Corinthians 9:24-25
Know ye not that they which run in a race run all, but one receives the prize? So run, that ye may obtain.
And every man that striveth for the mastery is temperate in all things. now they do it to obtain a corruptible crown; but we an incorruptible. KJV
You've all been to the stadium and seen the athletes race. Everyone runs; one wins. Run to win. All good athletes train hard. They do it for a gold medal that tarnishes and fades. You're after one that's gold eternally. The Message

If you are striving for the mastery, or the gold, you are temperate or disciplined in all things. Don't sell this race short. It is the most important race of your life. You can go out for track or a marathon if you'd like. However, the training is intense, well if you want to win that is. So also for this race. Your training is intense. Life is short. Follow Me. Read of the nature of Me and how I lived the human life as recorded in the four gospels. Learn about Me. Emulate Me. Discipline your life with morning prayer and seek Me. This will ensure you 'bring home the gold'!

October 18

Proverbs 14:24
The crown of the wise is their riches: but the foolishness of fools is folly. KJV
The wise accumulate wisdom; fools get stupider by the day.
The Message

When you tell them that is a wrong decision, you watch them cringe, and they still run with that decision anyways. Then you anguish as you witness the display of the fool. No, you cannot run everyone else's lives. However, you can learn from them. When they cringed, it was because they knew you were right, but they are unteachable. That's the fool - unteachable. When you are corrected - what's your reaction? To accumulate wisdom, you must be teachable. Humbleness is a trait of a teachable person. If you're not sure you agree with a correction you receive - tuck it away - ponder it - and ask Me. I'm pretty faithful about letting you know if you're doing wrong. Many times, I put people in your path to correct you. Always strive to do better. Don't walk around condemned. That isn't healthy either. Let Me use the resources in your life, the commodities if you will, of people. Let Me build you. I need you to be wise so that you can in turn work with others.

October 19

Proverbs 12:4
A virtuous woman is a crown to her husband: but she that maketh ashamed is as rottenness in his bones.   KJV

A hearty wife invigorates her husband, but a frigid woman is cancer in the bones.   The Message

If you could set your heart to love your husband, I can invigorate and bring life to him. He needs a wife that helps him. He took you as a spouse with a promise to love and honor you, to cover you, to provide for you, forsaking all others. He promised 'Me' that, and I have held him to it. Times and circumstances have brought to light the shortcomings of the human being that he is. However, he has not forgotten his promise. He still strives to keep it. You made Me some promises as well when you took him as your husband. If you would love him, it would make it so much easier for him. Look past the faults and the bad attitudes and see Me standing behind him. Let's encourage him today. Watch how you shine - right along with him.

October 20

Revelation 2:10
Fear none of those things which thou shalt suffer: behold, the devil shall cast some of you into prison, that ye may be tried; and ye shall have tribulation ten days: be thou faithful unto death, and I will give thee a crown of life. KJV

Tribulations and temptations are part of your spiritual warfare on earth. Look past them and straight at Me. I have your way through and out. When confused on the way to go - the decision to make - stand and pray. Never will I not answer. Always will I speak. Just wait and look for Me. Speak life and faith into the situation. Watch your circumstances change right before you. The crown of life is a real reward. Eternity holds this crown. Jesus promised you life and life more abundantly even on the earth. Walk My way and you will experience these things.

James 1:12
Blessed is the man that endureth temptation: for when he is tried, he shall receive the crown of life, which the Lord hath promised to them that love him.   KJV

John 14:21
He that hath my commandments, and keepeth them, he it is that loveth me:...   KJV

October 21

2 Chronicles 17:3
And the Lord was with Jehoshaphat, because he walked in the first ways of his father David, and sought not unto Baalim;   KJV

He looked and followed David's first steps, not David's mistakes. Jehoshaphat rejected idolatry and disobedience. He had a need. He needed to break a family curse. He made a deliberate choice. I don't want my past to determine my future. He looked for the good influences, not the bad ones. He made a decision. "I'm not going to follow evil." When you are walking through your life, if you would but stop and look at the circumstances. Next make deliberate decisions to change the circumstances. Then I can help you. This will not only help you break family curses and patterns of bad behavior in your life, but this will also 'create' a pattern of blessings for you.

October 22

2 Chronicles 17:4
But sought to the Lord God of his father, and walked in his commandments, and not after the doings of Israel. KJV

Your life has negative reference points. Jehoshaphat's father was one in his life. But Jehoshaphat didn't follow the rest of his family, who was the tribe of Israel, nor his father. He followed David's first steps. He decided in his life he wanted to be a leader in right instead of a follower of wrong. Look at your life. These negative reference points take the shape of divorces, abandonment, addictions, anger and abuse. These behaviors can be passed on down the family line. Bad behavior has a far-reaching effect. Following bad examples just doesn't make sense. Why would someone want to repeat destructive actions? It ends up looking like an epidemic in many families. That's because it is a spiritual issue. You can become the thing you hate. You must make a deliberate decision to follow what is right. You must come to Me and repent. You must learn My Word and follow My commandments. Seek Me, and wise counsel. These acts of obedience will alter your actions and your entire life forever. I want to help you to be an overcomer.

3 John 11
Beloved, follow not that which is evil, but that which is good.
He that doeth good is of God; but he that doeth evil hath not seen God.   KJV

October 23

2 Chronicles 17:6
And his heart was lifted up in the ways of the Lord: moreover he took away the high places and groves out of Judah.   KJV

He was single-minded in following God;
and he got rid of the local sex-and-religion shrines.   The Message

Use some wisdom and take personal responsibility. Look at your reference points and move towards them. The seasoned traveler in the woods or wilderness uses reference points - keeps one eye on it - moves toward it, and never gets lost. The one who does not, travels in circles, never seen again. Engineers seek the post, the reference point, in the ground and on the drawings before erecting a building. Without consulting and finding this reference point first, the building would be off, flawed, and uninhabitable. Use the Word as your reference point. Take the time and energy. Seek Me. Seek My ways. Direct your words at the things of Mine. It's very dishonest to ask and then not do what I say. Ask in prayer, 'God, what is hurting my relationship with you? What frustrates my walk with you?' Jehoshaphat wasn't doing the popular thing at the time. He was doing the right thing. He removed the obstacles between him and Me. He built a solid rock foundation for his life.

Hebrews 6:12
*That ye be not slothful, but followers of them who through faith
and patience inherit the promises. KJV*

*Don't drag your feet. Be like those who stay the course with
committed faith and then get everything promised to them.
The Message*

2 Chronicles 17:7, 9
*Also in the third year of his reign he sent to his princes .... to teach
in the cities of Judah.*

*And they taught in Judah, and had the book of the law of the Lord
with them, and went about throughout all the cities of Judah, and
taught the people. KJV*

Jehoshaphat understood for his people to live the Word, they must
hear it, and be taught it. There was a loss of joy, a dryness. That is a
sign of a lack of nearness to Me. When you experience this in your
life you must deliberately make time for the reading and learning of
the Word. Pray and ask for the return of the passion. Make My Word
and My commandments a part of your life. It has to go beyond just
reading a verse of scripture here and there. Seek Me. Line up your
faith. Learn and live Jesus Christ. This is life. This is life more
abundantly.

James 4:8
*Draw nigh to God, and he will draw nigh to you. Cleanse your
hands, ye sinners; and purify your hearts, ye double minded. KJV*

2 Chronicles 17:5, 12, 10
*Therefore the Lord stablished the kingdom in his hand; and all
Judah brought to Jehoshaphat presents; and he had riches and
honour in abundance.*

And Jehoshaphat waxed great exceedingly; ...

And the fear of the Lord fell upon all the kingdoms of the lands that were round about Judah so that they made no war against Jehoshaphat. KJV

Living for Me, is more than just - 'don't do bad'. When you make a deliberate decision to follow Me, you open the door to a pattern of blessings from My throne. I will make you solid and permanent. You will find favor with Me -- that others never find. Dominion and protection will follow you all your days. I bring provision to you -- to bring My will to pass in your life. This is all spiritual. It's My Spirit inside of you that comes alive and brings your spirit a vision for the kingdom. Others around you will catch that vision, as you live for Me. I'll prepare you for life's battles and I will use you to make an impact in other lives as well. Your influence will cause them to seek that same preparation for their life battles. Jehoshaphat made deliberate decisions to live for Me. This caused the pattern of blessing in his life. Those around Jehoshaphat stood and fought for him, not against him. This is a kingdom principle.

2 Chronicles 17:15
And next to him was Jehohanan the captain, and with him two hundred and four score thousand. KJV

October 26

James 1:13
Let no man say when he is tempted, I am tempted of God: for God cannot be tempted with evil, neither tempted he any man KJV

Don't let anyone under pressure to give in to evil say, "God is trying to trip me up." God is impervious to evil, and puts evil in no one's way. The Message

I do not tempt you. Mark it down. Memorize it. I do not. The devil does. He is your enemy. Keep a clear picture of him in your brain. This exposes your weaknesses when he does. He goes for your weak points. He's a master at studying you and knowing the areas to tempt you in. He's seeking that vulnerability in you. He wants to rip you off. He constantly looks for your price, the price that will cause you to fall. These are chinks in your armor. When you are tempted, pick up your head. Take notice of the area he is hitting you in. Job didn't deny Me. He stayed prayed up. Peter did. He slept through prayer meeting. Let the temptation take you to prayer. I can help you. I will show you the way to overcome and escape. If you fall, repent and get back up. But even if you repent after falling, he's coming back again with the exact same temptation. Because you've shown it's your weakness. Your only way of overcoming it, is to resist the devil and he will flee. When you've done all to stand, just stand! You have to pray, so you can resist through Me, and stand through Me. That's why Christ died. To give you the cutting edge, the relationship with Me. You might as well fight the battle today, if you keep falling, he takes more ground, and it'll be a tougher fight for you the next time. This is spiritual warfare. Your weakness is in sin, your strength is in Me.

October 27

Psalms 91:1
He that dwellest in the secret place of the most High shall abide
under the shadow of the Almighty.   KJV

When you meet with Me, I shadow you. My covering will shield you, and deliver you. As you find your place of refuge in Me, your trust will grow and grow. If you never enter this secret place, you will never experience this covering. My covering obliterates fear. My shadow, as your habitation, provides a safety like no other. Angels will minister, and bear you up in their hands. You'll trample enemies with victory. I have set My love on you. Have you set yours on Me?

October 28

Psalms 18:29
For by thee I have run through a troop; and by my God have I
leaped over a wall.   KJV

Suddenly, God, you floodlight my life; I'm blazing with glory,
God's glory!
I smash the bands of marauders, I vault the highest fences. What a
God!   The Message

Always remember your strength comes from Me. You won't be jumping any walls without first starting your days in morning prayer.

That kind of strength comes from a relationship with Me. Few there are that take time for Me. That's why I call you a peculiar person, one after My own heart, if you will wake and find time for Me. And if you will obey Me and My Word to boot? Oh, how I could tear down strongholds in your life! David experienced the blazing glory of his God, because of his prayer life. He did find that spot in Me, that secret place, that closet prayer life. Have you?

October 29

Proverbs 12:25
Heaviness in the heart of man maketh it stoop: but a good word
maketh it glad.   KJV
Worry weighs us down; a cheerful word picks us up.
The Message

Words are powerful! I cannot stress that enough. When you speak worry, you will live worry, and heaviness will ensue, and the heart being heavy will cause your countenance to fall, and your body to stoop, or be weighed down. Light hearted folks, are not light hearted because everything always goes right. Light hearted folks, are light hearted because they speak cheerfulness. Many times, this rubs salt in the wounds of the heavy hearted. I am not saying run around rubbing salt in everyone's wounds. I am saying, if you want to make someone happy, speak something cheerful. There are times to mourn, times for anger, times for seriousness, but not every moment of your life. There comes a time for joy, and a time to rebuild and time for cheer. Foresee enough, be wise enough, perceptive enough – to know when it's ok to speak some words of cheer. However, always, always, always speak words of faith. The cheer will come. Speak, "God is good." This turns the page.

October 30

John 14:26
But the Comforter; which is the Holy Ghost, whom the Father will
send in my name, he shall teach you all things, and bring all things
to your remembrance, whatsoever I have said unto you.   KJV

The Friend, the Holy Spirit whom the Father will send at my
request, will make everything plain to you. He will remind you of

all the things I have told you. I'm leaving you well and whole.
That's my parting gift to you.   The Message

When My Son was taken back to heaven I did not leave you alone.
Never on earth did man have the Holy Spirit to indwell in them.
This miracle needed the sacrifice, the death and the resurrection of
Christ to take place first. I could not dwell in anyone amongst sin.
The blood of Christ washes away the sin in the surrendered heart.
As you strive to live for Me, repent daily, come and lay your sins at
the altar, it is part of the plan of salvation. When Jesus taught you to
pray, He taught you this. Meet with Me in your mornings, Christ did
every morning at 4 am. How much more should you? Begin your
day with Me. As I indwell in you – My presence will be
unmistakably felt throughout your day. Not that faith needs
'feelings'. I just want to make Myself known to you. When it seems,
I am far away – pull aside – break away from the crowd – and spend
some time in My Word. Take a step towards Me and I will draw
close to you, and bring you peace in the chaos. This is a kingdom
access that only Mine have. This is fellowship with Me.

October 31

Roman road
3:23, 6:23, 5:8,10:9-10,10:13

Romans 3:23

For all have sinned, and come short of the glory of God;   KJV

> **Since we've compiled this long and sorry record as**
> **sinners (both us and them) and proved that we are utterly**
> **incapable of living the glorious lives God wills for us, God**
> **did it for us.   The Message**

Romans 6:23
For the wages of sin is death; but the gift of God is eternal life
through Jesus Christ our Lord. KJV

> **Work hard for sin your whole life and your pension is**
> **death. But God's gift is real life, eternal life, delivered by**
> **Jesus, our Master.   The Message**

Romans 5:8

But God commendeth his love toward us, in that, while we were yet sinners, Christ died for us. KJV

> But God put his love on the line for us by offering his Son in sacrificial death while we were of no use whatever to him.   The Message

Romans 10:9-10
That if thou shalt confess with thy mouth the Lord Jesus, and shalt believe in thine heart that God hath raised him from the dead, thou shalt be saved.
For with the heart man believeth unto righteousness; and with the mouth confession is made unto salvation.   KJV

> The word that saves is right here, as near as the tongue in your mouth, as close as the heart in your chest. It's the word of faith that welcomes God to go to work and set things right for us. This is the core of our preaching. Say the welcoming word to God – "Jesus is my Master" – embracing, body and soul, God's work of doing in us what he did in raising Jesus from the dead. That's it. You're not "doing" anything; you're simply calling out to God, trusting him to do it for you. That's salvation. With your whole being you embrace God setting things right, and then you say it, right out loud: "God has set everything right between him and me!"   The Message

Romans 10:13
For whosoever shall call upon the name of the Lord shall be saved.

> "Everyone who calls, 'Help, God!' gets help."
> The Message

It would do you well to memorize my Word, so you can lead someone to Christ. Lead someone who is interested through these scriptures. I will move and stir them. I will draw them. Their life will change forever. My Word never returns void.

NOVEMBER

November 1

Psalms 9:1
I will praise thee, O Lord, with my whole heart; I will shew forth
all thy marvelous works.
I will be glad and rejoice in thee: I will sing praise to thy name, O
thou Most High.
When mine enemies are turned back, they shall fall and perish at
thy presence.   KJV

I'm thanking you, God, from a full heart, I'm writing the book on
your wonders.
I'm whistling, laughing, and jumping for joy; I'm singing your
song, High God.
The day my enemies turned tail and ran, they stumbled on you and
fell on their faces.   The Message

I truly do protect Mine. My will for your life includes many trials and temptations, just because you live in a fallen world. I am with you as you navigate this gospel road. Let Me plan your days, then you follow. This is where your joy is. I can't explain it in human words. Trust and follow, then watch what happens. Your insides will burst with joy – that's your soul - filled with Me. As you trust and follow – you draw closer to Me. Your enemies can't touch that. As you walk in obedience, nothing can separate you from the love of Me. This is a kingdom principle.

November 2

Psalms 50:14-15
Offer unto God thanksgiving; and pay thy vows unto the most High:
And call upon me in the day of trouble; I will deliver thee, and thou shalt glorify me.   KJV

"Spread for me a banquet of praise, serve High God a feast of kept promises,
And call for help when you're in trouble – I'll help you, and you'll honor me."   The Message

As you enter this holiday season, take time to reflect on the spirit of thanksgiving in your heart. That is a part of My nature, manifesting in you. Thanksgiving is a natural response to love and relationship with another. It's not just the spoken word, although that is critical to the listening ear, it is also the attitude of the giver. If someone said thank you, under their breath and with sarcasm and zero respect or honor, it is of course not well received. It does little to open doors and further the relationship with anyone, let alone allow you the heart to help that person when they are in need the next time. Remember who you are speaking with when you offer your thanksgiving. If it is someone you could really care less about, then how could you expect any response at all? If it is someone you hold in high regard, and believe to be your Father in heaven, and the Savior of your soul, guard your attitude, no matter what the circumstances. Ask Me – if you need help with your moodiness - I can do that.

November 3

Psalms 100:4
Enter into his gates with thanksgiving, and into his courts with
praise: be thankful unto him, and bless his name.
For the Lord is good; his mercy is everlasting; and his truth
endureth to all generations.   KJV

Enter with the password: "Thank you!" Make yourselves at home,
talking praise. Thank him. Worship him.
For God is sheer beauty, all-generous in love, loyal always and
ever.   The Message

When Jesus taught you to pray He taught you to enter My courts
with praise. Whenever approaching the throne, take time to
approach with praise. This shows humility, respect, dignity and
reverence, towards Me, your God and Creator. This opens up
dialogue that cannot be opened any other way. My desire to bless
you is beyond words, My mercy on you cannot be compared, My
loyalty will endure forever. As you enter My courts with praise you
display in the spiritual realm that you are a child of Mine. I am
sovereign, I have authority far beyond any earthly king. I am able to
do exceedingly and abundantly above all things. Share your prayer
with Me. I'm on the edge of My seat, bending and waiting to hear.

November 4

Colossians 3:15
And let the peace of God rule in your hearts, to the which also ye
are called in one body; and be ye thankful.   KJV

Let the peace of Christ keep you in tune with each other, in step
with each other. None of this going off and doing your own thing.
And cultivate thankfulness.   The Message

When you are counting your blessings, and bringing thanksgiving,
do not forget to be thankful for each other in Christ Jesus. He is the
head of the body, your brothers and sisters are a part of the body, just
as you are. Don't walk around and forget to bring them a word of
encouragement and a conversation that thanks them for their

faithfulness as well. Would you last long as an arm cut off and thrown over there? How many nice days would there be as a leg cut off and thrown over here? It is the body operating together that brings unity and harmony to the kingdom. Jesus is blessed and encouraged when you work together for a common goal as He has called you. As you make your goals to be in the winning of souls – all of heaven rejoices. If you know that over one soul heaven gets excited, you should see us when the body makes it a priority and moves towards that together. That is peace for your heart you won't find any other way.

November 5

1 Chronicles 29:12-13
Both riches and honour come of thee, and thou reignest over all; and in thine hand is power and might; and in thine hand it is to make great, and to give strength unto all.
Now therefore, our God, we thank thee, and praise thy glorious name.
But who am I…?   KJV

As My Son gave His life, you through repentance became a child of Mine. That's who you are. As you lift up holy hands, and bring thankfulness and praise unto My Name, you are drawn closer to Me. You see the change in your life is only because of Jesus Christ and His sacrifice on Calvary's cross. Your riches, your honor, your strength, your power, it all comes from Me. However, sin stopped the flow into your life. I could not move because I cannot be in the presence of sin. His sacrifice covers your sin. Your repentance is key to this. As you repent, My Spirit has right into your life. An indwelling of My Spirit in you changes and revolutionizes your life. You are no longer a slave to sin, nor fear. You have been redeemed. Take time and think on these things. Salvation is incredible. Eternity will last forever, and Mine will dwell in My house with Me for all of eternity.

November 6

1 Chronicles 16:8-11
Give thanks unto the Lord, call upon his name, make known his deeds among the people.

HE KNOWS MY NAME

Sing unto him, sing psalms unto him, talk ye of all his wondrous works.
Glory ye in his holy name: let the heart of them rejoice that seek the Lord.
Seek the Lord and his strength, seek his face continually.   KJV

Those that seek Me will find Me. Those that don't, just won't. Seek My face continually, seek it with praise and worship, songs and spoken words. Words are powerful and I inhabit the praises of My people. Draw close to Me and I will draw close to you. I want to strengthen you, meet with Me, let Me lift those burdens and encourage your life today. When you're feeling down, put on the spirit of praise, it will break the spirit of heaviness. Even your shoulders will lift. You'll be astounded and full of joy in the midst of the trial.

November 7

Psalms 107:1
O give thanks unto the Lord, for he is good: for his mercy endureth for ever.
Let the redeemed of the Lord say so, whom he hath redeemed from the hand of the enemy   KJV

Oh, thank God – he's so good! His love never runs out.
All of you set free by God, tell the world! Tell how he freed you from oppression   The Message

As you testify and give thanks of My hand moving in your life, your friend's and colleague's heads will lift up, their ears will listen, even when they appear not to. My Word never returns void. Use scripture whenever you can when speaking to them. This is the sowing of the seed. You don't have to quote the chapter and verse number for My Word to penetrate. Simply speak, "Praise God – He's so good to me," "Jesus changed me, because of His forgiveness in my life, I am not bound by alcohol anymore, could we use an eatery that doesn't serve alcohol this time?" "God spoke to me to give you this, I hope you can use it." "May I bless the food before we eat?" Make it a part of your life. Speaking of Me and what I have done for you. This is also the watering of the seed. Say, "I'm sorry you're sick, may I pray for you? God healed me the other day when I prayed. Let's see what God will do." Step out in faith. Let them know that you know Me and that is what makes a difference in you. I want to reach them. Tell them, "Jesus died for you. You don't have to go through this alone. Would you like to surrender your life and all of these trials to Him? I'll pray with you if you'd like. God changed me, He can change you." That is the reaping of the harvest. Be My hands and feet, that's your calling.

November 8

Colossians 1:11-12

Strengthened with all might, according to his glorious power, unto all patience and longsuffering with joyfulness;

Giving thanks unto the Father which hath made us meet to be partakers of the inheritance of the saints in light;   KJV

It is strength that endures the unendurable and spills over into joy, thanking the Father who makes us strong enough to take part in everything bright and beautiful that he has for us.

The Message

Your inheritance is a powerful thing. Your inheritance is in the light of Christ, the light of the saints is Christ. As I have delivered you from the powers of darkness and set you up in the kingdom of My Son, you have received an inheritance. Never take it lightly. It was blood-bought. Always remember the forgiveness of your sins was blood-bought. Your inheritance gives you the strength of all might and glorious power and patience and longsuffering which becomes your joy unspeakable. Run in that. Do not allow hell to deceive you into weakness and lameness and hard-heartedness. As you bring the sacrifice of praise and thanksgiving - your brightness and beauty will outshine any hardship you are enduring. Keep your eyes on Me, on your inheritance. Jesus is the light of the world, He is the light at the end of the tunnel. Eyes forward, think of heaven.

November 9

Psalms 103:2

Bless the Lord, O my soul, and forget not all his benefits   KJV

Take time to detail in your mind the blessings of life. Say, "I am thankful for ...," and fill in the blanks. As you do this and look about you for the rich blessings to detail from My throne into your home, your family, and your life – you will feel the burdens and weights of the world lift from your physical body. You are a physical body - but you are also a spiritual body. If you would tap into the spiritual laws I have set in motion, you will tap into a physical healing. Sore, run down, weary, heavy laden? As you look for, and give thanks for, the blessings that you have received, your physical body will be restored. Give thanks, have a thankful heart, have a giving spirit, take time for others, look at it as an opportunity to witness to someone when you see a need and fulfill it. Always, always share the hope of Christ, and point them towards the window of hope in the cross. Don't forget all I've done for you, and never neglect to share it with others.

November 10

Psalms 136:26

O give thanks unto the God of heaven: for his mercy endureth for ever.   KJV

Thank God, who did it all! His love never quits!   The Message

I formed you in the palm of My hands. I did that because I have a reason and a purpose for your life. As you enter into thanksgiving and lift up your hands, those palms I gave to you, I will fill them with wisdom and hope beyond your wildest imagination. As you walk in faith, and believe Me for those promises I give you, they will come to pass. Hope realized. I want to bless your life more than you will ever realize. So -- lift up those hands, worship and praise, be thankful for the small things. I want to fill you today.

November 11

Ephesians 5:20

Giving thanks always for all things unto God and the Father in the name of our Lord Jesus Christ;

Submitting yourselves one to another in the fear of God.   KJV

Sing songs from your heart to Christ. Sing praises over everything, any excuse for a song to God the Father in the name of our Master, Jesus Christ.   The Message

Having trouble with submission? Take time to worship, sing songs. When you sing songs of praise and worship this will usher in My presence. As My presence is ushered into your life you will be able to follow My commands with much less resistance of the flesh. Submission is an incredible outlet for you and your mind. Your conflict in the mind, and condemnation comes from carrying loads you have no business carrying. When you leave those loads to your headship, then you can be about your lighter load and enjoy the weights being lifted from your shoulders. Your growth depends on it. Would you lay a full pack on the back of a child? Would you give an old woman your groceries to carry? Would you give a teenager your budget to figure out? Would you tell your problems to the man next door who has just lost his son? None of these circumstances would make sense. Neither does it make sense for you to carry a load that only your headship has been designed to carry. Take time to sing some beautiful worship songs today. Leave the worldly songs packed away. They celebrate sin and misery and create an ugly environment that will leave your soul wanting. I want to bless your life, come, fellowship with Me.

November 12

Philippians 1:3-6

I thank my God upon every remembrance of you,

Always in every prayer of mine for you all making request with joy,

For your fellowship in the gospel from the first day until now;

Being confident of this very thing, that he which hath begun a good work in you will perform it until the day of Jesus Christ KJV

Every time you cross my mind, I break out in exclamations of thanks to God.   The Message

It would do you well to pray for the folks that were there for you when you first got saved. Some have strayed from the faith. Some are still there. Encourage them with your own testimony of their fruitfulness in the Kingdom. Let them know how I am still moving in your life, because they took the time for you in your early days of salvation. Pray and contend for them. Your prayers are powerful and can change a situation and the course of their lives. I want to bless them, as they have blessed you. Move mountains for them, just because you can, through Me.

November 13

Psalms 18:46, 49

The Lord liveth; and blessed be my rock; and let the God of my salvation be exalted.

Therefore will I give thanks unto thee, O Lord, among the heathen and sing praises unto thy name.   KJV

That's why I'm thanking you, God, all over the world. That's why I'm singing songs that rhyme your name.   The Message

If you will give praise and testify of My miracles to those around you, sinner or saint, this will exalt My name and build My kingdom. The words you speak create an atmosphere around you. You want your family saved? You want your workmates to be born again? I hear you pray for them each morning from your prayer list. As I have moved and placed a seed in their hearts and minds from those prayers, it is time for you to water the seed with a testimony of how I am moving in your life. Share the details of one of your small answered prayers, and the privilege of a sound mind and healed body because of salvation through Jesus Christ. Don't rush through the conversation, be confident, and give them a few moments of lingering in My presence as you speak. The psalmist reminds you to sing songs of praise and worship in their midst. It doesn't always have to be musical, you can speak of the things of the kingdom as well. Make My Name a household word amongst you. Watch how I change things.

November 14

Psalms 18:30

What a God! His road stretches straight and smooth.

Every God – direction is road – tested. Everyone who runs toward him makes it.   The Message

As for God, his way is perfect: the word of the Lord is tried;

he is a buckler to all those that trust in him.   KJV

My ways are perfect, because I am perfect. You can trust that. When the psalmist used the word buckler he was conveying to you the shield that comes to your life when you simply trust in Me. You will make it. You will more than just make it. This is the way that leads to eternal life. This is the way that leads to life more abundantly. If you will trust in what I say, and that means acting on when I ask you to do something, I will shield you in times of trouble. It's an absolute law of nature. I cannot lie, because I am God. When you trust in Me – you receive from Me. Use My road, it's a great adventure. Wonderful destiny and purpose line the road to heaven. Let Me shield you, put your trust on!

November 15

Psalms 18:3

I will call upon the Lord, who is worthy to be praised; so shall I be saved from mine enemies. KJV

Spiritual warfare is a topic you love. You know why you love it? Because you're Mine. I created you with a heart to fight. People who lay down their swords never see a victory. Of course, I am talking about the sword of the Spirit, which is the Word of God. Praise is a very important tool in your arsenal of weapons. When you praise and worship – demons flee. Pure and simple fact. When you mope and groan and complain that you don't have things your 'own' way – you feed the enemy and give them huge open doors into your life through the gaps in your armor. Lift up your hands every day and worship. Try it right now if you haven't already this morning. Do you see the difference in your countenance? Lift up your voice to heaven, praise and glorify the King of kings and Lord of lords. Thank Jesus, out loud, for His sacrifice on Calvary for your precious salvation. This throws hell into a tail spin. You are on the offense -- not the defense today. Fight. Do not lay down your sword for any distraction. Your spiritual warfare is critical to those you pray for and for yourself. Take time in your bible. I want to move the enemy out of your way today.

Psalms 18:34

He teacheth my hands to war, so that a bow of steel is broken by mine arms. KJV

Psalms 118:21

I will praise thee: for thou hast heard me, and art become my salvation. KJV

Thank you for responding to me; you've truly become my salvation! The Message

Hope realized is an amazing thing. Every human heart longs and hopes. Despair comes when the hope is not realized. Heaviness encloses and encases the heart and creates a hardness that few can break free from. The hope I give, in answered prayer, is a lightening of the heart. It brings a joy to the spirit and a song to the lips. The hope I give brings light to the eye and peace to the mind. As you see Me respond to prayer take time for thanksgiving. When you don't see the response you thought you needed, take time for thanksgiving anyways. Your salvation is true, and My grace surely is sufficient for you. A delay does not necessarily mean a 'no'. Always park that in the back of your mind. And park this in the front of your mind, thanksgiving opens the door for the next hope realized.

Colossians 4:2,12

Continue in prayer, and watch in the same with thanksgiving

Epaphras, who is one of you, a servant of Christ, saluteth you, always laboring fervently for you in prayers, that ye may stand perfect and complete in all the will of God.   KJV

Pray diligently. Stay alert, with your eyes wide open in gratitude.

Epaphras, who is one of you, says hello. What a trooper he has been! He's been tireless in his prayers for you, praying that you'll stand firm, mature and confident in everything God wants you to do.   The Message

As you pray, look about you and remember to be thankful for the answered prayers. Because I will answer your prayers. Pray for one another. Prayer moves circumstances. You will see situations that need a hand of God to remedy. It is your responsibility to contend for your brothers and sisters in the faith. Pray for My complete will in their lives so they can stand as they should. As you fight in the spiritual realm for each other, you will grow as a congregation and as a community. You will see yourselves become stones, fitly formed together, to make a beautiful structure that will cause all of the saints to be amazed.

November 18

Psalms 118:17-19

I shall not die, but live, and declare the works of the Lord.

The Lord hath chastened me sore; but he hath not given me over unto death.

Open to me the gates of righteousness; I will go into them, and I will praise the Lord   KJV

I didn't die. I lived! And now I'm telling the world what God did.

God tested me, he pushed me hard, but he didn't hand me over to Death.

Swing wide the city gates – the righteous gates! I'll walk right through and thank God!   The Message

Many days will come when you believe you have more on your plate than you can handle. Many days it is a sword, to fight hell, in one hand, and a trowel, to build your home, in the other. Many days it will seem so overwhelming that you cannot believe one more shoe dropped, and you are not sure how to handle this last issue. When you feel this way, when the mind seems clouded, it could be your own doing. You may have made a mess of things. It may be a chastening from My throne into your life. But no matter what the circumstance, or the reason, look to Me. Make it a habit. Ask Me for direction, and I will always always always give you a way out. You'll sometimes do it so much that it seems to be a habit forming. But it's not a bad habit to be in. It's a lifesaving habit as a matter of fact. Come to Me with a thankful heart, I want to give you that victory!

November 19

Psalms 118:28-29

Thou art my God, and I will praise thee: thou art my God, I will exalt thee.

O give thanks unto the Lord; for he is good: for his mercy endureth for ever.   KJV

You're my God, and I thank you. O my God, I lift high your praise. Thank God – he's so good. His love never quits!   The Message

Pick up your head, straighten your neck, straighten your back. Put on My strength. My mercies in your life endure forever and ever and ever. That is what eternity is, for ever. The trials and situations you are enduring today will not last but a second in time compared to the blessings of heaven. Trust Me in these things that seem to engulf you at the moment. The devil is a liar. You are not so consumed that I cannot help you. Even a child remembers to say, "I can always ask God for help." Take time and ask Me for help.

Enter My courts with praise, and move the obstacles that keep you from the strength and mercy of My hand. Come in humble, that's the key to being lifted up when you leave.

Colossians 2:6-7

As you have therefore received Christ Jesus the Lord, so walk ye in him: Rooted and built up in him, and stablished in the faith, as ye have been taught, abounding therein with thanksgiving. KJV

My counsel for you is simple and straightforward: Just go ahead with what you've been given. You received Christ Jesus, the Master; now live him. You're deeply rooted in him. You're well constructed upon him. You know your way around the faith. Now do what you've been taught. School's out; quit studying the subject and start living it! And let your living spill over into thanksgiving. The Message

It's great to study, it helps build wisdom. Understanding comes from prayer. Now put those to use, in a life lived for Christ. The world, and your enemy, tends to sway and coerce you into believing that there is no reason to change your habits. My Word tells you completely different. Read it, and do it. Do not just be a hearer of My Word, but be a doer of My Word. This will change more circumstances than you could ever hope for. This will cut down on your need for advice from others and winding yourself up into a frenzy over trials and tribulations. I am not saying that they all will disappear. You live on the earth, there will be challenges and obstacles that will build and strengthen you -- until My Son's return. However, you will be able to walk through, around, over and stomp on anything the devil and the world throw your way. Discipline your life, cut the ties and the bridges to the old life. Live for Christ. You can do this with a delighted thankful heart. You are no longer a slave to sins, addictions, or people who want to trip you up and rip you off from your destiny in heaven.

Colossians 2:7 ...abounding therein with thanksgiving. KJV

Philippians 4:6-7

Be careful for nothing; but in every thing by prayer and supplication with thanksgiving let your requests be made know unto God.

And the peace of God, which passeth all understanding, shall keep your hearts and minds through Christ Jesus. KJV

Don't fret or worry. Instead of worrying, pray. Let petitions and praises shape your worries into prayers, letting God know your concerns.

Before you know it, a sense of God's wholeness, everything coming together for good, will come and settle you down. It's wonderful what happens when Christ displaces worry at the center of your life.   The Message

When you use thanksgiving and praise in your requests before My throne, a peace will physically come into your heart, and into your mind, because it is through Christ Jesus, who inhabits the praises of My people. That is not a light word, inhabit. He dwells within you. As you praise, He floods in. As He floods in, peace wonderfully settles inside of you, with the evidence being in your heart and in your mind. All the rest of the world and its care flow out, His Spirit takes control. Your human understanding – this side of heaven – won't comprehend it. Your worries and concerns that He will help you voice to Me will melt away. All things will work together for good, trust Me in that. As you do, you will settle down. Better than a great cup of coffee. I got the answer!!

November 22

Ephesians 6:18

Praying always with all prayer and supplication in the Spirit, and watching thereunto with all perseverance and supplication for all saints;   KJV

In the same way, prayer is essential in this ongoing warfare. Pray hard and long. Pray for your brothers and sisters. Keep your eyes open. Keep each other's spirits up so that no one falls behind or drops out.   The Message

When your days seem long and suddenly someone enters the room dripping with adversity, you will need to remember to pray and thank Me for the opportunity to minister to someone you have been praying for. Yes - she is trying to pick a fight, cause you to stumble, trip you up. Your discernment is correct. She wants to run and tell her friends -- you fell. However, you have been praying hard and long for her, just because she once served Me with all of her heart. You see she has strayed from the faith and even lost her common sense, which is evident with the decisions she is making in her life. She begins to criticize the church and God's people. She says, "They say…." But it is really her saying it, look at her mouth moving. Keep your eyes open. Go in the other room for a moment if you need to. Recognize the enemy for who he is. Recognize the poor soul that is falling, for who she is. Ask Me, and I will give you the words for correction and instruction to speak into her life, and all the while, bring your requests with thankfulness for the opportunity to serve and to persevere for another sister in the midst of her lashing out at Me. It is no coincidence, the devil will bring the very ones who you pray for, to try and destroy you, but also to destroy your relationship with them. So that in unforgiveness, you will begin to not pray for them anymore.   This is a battle in your ongoing warfare. Stay thankful, enter My courts with praise, every morning. Stay prayed up. You must be ready with this part of your armor – put it on all of the time.

November 23

Ephesians 2:8-9

For by grace are ye saved through faith; and that not of yourselves: it is the gift of God:

Not of works, lest any man should boast.   KJV

Saving is all his idea, and all his work. All we do is trust him enough to let him do it. It's God's gift from start to finish!

We don't play the major role. If we did, we'd probably go around bragging that we'd done the whole thing! No, we neither make nor save ourselves. God does both the making and saving.
The Message

When you are given a gift, the proper response is to say, "Thank you." Thanksgiving is something the president of the United States, A. Lincoln, (and G. Washington as well) understood would move and bless a nation drowning in turmoil and war. Blood-stained, the people of the nation came to Me in a day set aside, not for false religious reasons, but a day set aside to cry out to Me to heal their land. They thanked Me for My gifts, for My mercy and asked Me to restore My purpose for this nation. That is evidence of a thankful heart, and a heart that recognized the hand of his God moving in his nation. Do you have that heart? Do you have that vision in your own life, where you see the hand of your God moving and changing things, His mercy and gifts flowing from heaven to you in the midst of your trials and circumstances? I give you many gifts, salvation is the most precious. Take time for thanksgiving and worship -- for this gift of salvation -- no matter what went wrong with your life today, take time. This is a spiritual key to the restoration of your life.

November 24

Psalms 28:7

The Lord is my strength and my shield; my heart trusted in him, and I am helped: therefore my heart greatly rejoiceth; and with my song will I praise him.   KJV

He proved he's on my side; I've thrown my lot in with him. Now I'm jumping for joy, and shouting and singing my thanks to him. The Message

I am your strength and shield. You do well to trust in Me. I am where your help comes from. When you pray, pray with the confidence of knowing this. This is not only where I can move, this is where you can see the miracles plain as day, and know without a doubt that it is Me. If you cannot pray with that confidence, take time in My Word. You need your faith strengthened. My Word is a living Word. It is not dead religion. My Word never returns empty or void. It is full of life. As you become acquainted with it, with Me, your confidence and faith will grow. Read and turn the pages, read them out loud, read them silently, read them in the morning, the afternoon and the evening. Fill up, take a good long read, and watch your spirit soar. Then pray for that miracle again, in the full confidence of Christ. See what I do!

Colossians 3:16-17

Let the word of Christ dwell in you richly in all wisdom; teaching and admonishing one another in psalms and hymns and spiritual songs, singing with grace in your hearts to the Lord.

And whatsoever ye do in word or deed, do all in the name of the Lord Jesus, giving thanks to God and the Father by him.   KJV

And cultivate thankfulness. Let the Word of Christ – The Message – have the run of the house. Give it plenty of room in your lives, Instruct and direct one another using good common sense. And sing, sing your hearts out to God!

Let every detail in your lives – words, actions, whatever – be done in the name of the Master, Jesus, thanking God the Father every step of the way.   The Message

How do you teach thankfulness? How do you cultivate it in your home, in the workplace, in your generation, amongst your family and peers, even in your own heart? Let Christ, let His Words dwell in you. Let them come out of you. Read them. Learn them. Memorize them. Write them on the tablet of your heart. Most of all, practice them. Remind each other with worship and praise, songs and joy, and delight each other with the Word of God. This cultivates thankfulness. If you want corn next year, you would plant corn seed. If you want a good crop you would care for it carefully. If not, you would neglect it. Same in the kingdom. Cultivate that thankfulness. Cultivate it with the Word of God. Watch it grow in your life and surroundings, then you may watch yourself grow as well as you are nourished and encouraged by this very thing.

1 Thessalonians 5:16-19

Rejoice evermore.

Pray without ceasing.

In every thing give thanks; for this is the will of God in Christ Jesus concerning you.

Quench not the Spirit.   KJV

Be cheerful no matter what; pray all the time; thank God no matter what happens. This is the way God wants you who belong to Christ Jesus to live. Don't suppress the Spirit.   The Message

You want My Spirit to reside in you? You want to have the fruits of My Spirit? The fruits are manifested in your behavior. Your behavior will never be altered until you learn to praise and worship and give thanks to the Lord your God. These things usher in My Spirit. Remember I told you about the words you speak? How powerful they are? Praise and worship and thanksgiving is power enabling, far beyond your understanding. Trust me on this. Walk in this. Give it six months, making it a changed behavior. Even in hard times, speak, "praise God." When the trial hits, speak, "I trust you God." It's great you have learned to bind the devil, and pull down strongholds. That's maturity for sure. Take the next step, even the first step. Worship. Praise and worship and thanksgiving, and watch Me move in the spiritual realm. You will look back in six months and see a markedly different character in yourself. You will also see many victories that could not have been won any other way but through Me. And there will be no doubt about it. That's kingdom dynamics manifesting in your life!

1 Chronicles 16:34

O give thanks unto the Lord; for he is good; for his mercy endureth for ever.   KJV

Give thanks to God – he is good and his love never quits. Say, "Save us, Savior God, round us up and get us out of these godless places, So we can give thanks to your holy Name, and bask in your life of praise." Blessed be God, the God of Israel, from everlasting to everlasting. Then everybody said, "Yes! Amen!" and "Praise God!"   The Message

If you can process life through praise and worship your life would change 180 degrees. You would change your route, change your clothes, and change your address. Your countenance would change so much, the people in your daily life would be astounded at the glow that flows from you. Your conversation would change to lightness and dignity and your mind would clear of all frustrations. When you surrendered your life to Me, I took control. With praise and worship you are reminded who really is in control. I told Paul 'it's hard to kick against the pricks'. I'll tell you the same. It's hard to live life when you are always kicking against Me, like a spoiled child being dragged out of the grocery store because they didn't get what they wanted. Could you give a child anything under those circumstances? Certainly not. Could you even give them a task to complete? Certainly not. You have to straighten out the control factor first. Could you bless them? No! So in you, stop kicking and fighting. Change your moaning into praise and thanksgiving and watch your world ignite around you with joy and peace.

Colossians 4:2

Continue in prayer, and watch in the same with thanksgiving; KJV

Be persistent and devoted to prayer, being alert and focused in your prayer life with an attitude of thanksgiving.   AMP

Whenever you pray keep an attitude of thanksgiving. Paul understood this, he was asking the church for prayer, and he desperately needed a prayer covering at the time. He wanted to reach people for Christ in the midst of, and in spite of his imprisonment. Not an easy task. Especially on his own. However, in his understanding, he knew the people in the church would be more concerned for his release, than My will. He was trying to convey that there was indeed something to be thankful for in this situation. Even though he was imprisoned he was concerned how the non-believers would view his faith. I was showing Paul the opportunity for souls there. He understood I wanted them to know Jesus. I was able to move many times for him in the spiritual realm because of the thankful heart he had in so many trying circumstances. People who knew Paul in the prisons were amazed and wanted to know the God of Paul, just because of his humble attitude and thankful heart. Do you have that? Do you have that in prayer? Do you have that in trials of life? Look around, I'm trying to reach the lost, and I'd like to use you to do it. Would you speak My Word to someone today? If you lack boldness, I can give that to you, when you pray with a thankful heart.

Psalms 118:14-15

The Lord is my strength and song, and is become my salvation.

The voice of rejoicing is in the tabernacles of the righteous: the right hand of the Lord doeth valiantly. KJV

God's my strength, he's also my salvation.

Hear the shouts, hear the triumph songs in the camp of the saved? The Message

The songs of victory and triumph comes from My people. Many times, it is by faith, while they are still in the battle and see no way out. Other times it erupts as they see the tide change against their enemy and for their dominion. You want to do valiantly? Act like a warrior. Raise your voice in praise and worship. Watch Me fight and win the battle. Glorify My Name. Lift up thanksgivings to your God. It will pull down the strongholds of the enemy. Raise up a standard as a righteous child of God. It will trample hell and its strategies under your feet. Always, always do what is right. When you fall - repent - and get back up in song through salvation.

November 30

Psalms 118:1

O give thanks unto the Lord; for he is good: because his mercies endureth forever. KJV

Thank God because he's good, because his love never quits.

The Message

My love for you never quits. I work constantly to keep you safe. You are My responsibility. You are Mine. I am your God. That makes Me responsible to teach, to nurture, and to provide and protect you. When you grasp that, your faith will swell. When you mature and get understanding in these things, you will move mountains in My name. Pick up your head, dust off the stress and worries with a song of praise and worship. Put the armor on, set your eyes forward and be about your Father's business. This will make you more than a conqueror.

DECEMBER

December 1

Jeremiah 6:27

I have set thee for a tower and a fortress among my people, that thou mayest know and try their way. KJV

God gave me this task: "I have made you the examiner of my people, to examine and weigh their lives. They're a thick headed, hard-nosed bunch, rotten to the core, the lot of them. Refining fires are cranked up to white heat, but the ore stays a lump, unchanged. It's useless to keep trying any longer. Nothing can refine evil out of them. Men will give up and call them 'slag,' thrown on the slag heap by me, their God.   The Message

There is a refining fire in your life that is critical to refine and change you. The evil comes out, the changing begins. If you refuse to change, it creates a person you really don't want to be. Evil creates a thick headed, hard-nose, nasty kind of person. Do you know any of those? Are you one of those? I want to keep working on you, but you must allow Me to remove the slag as it floats to the top. Whatever I'm dealing with you on, you'll know. That's the slag I'm speaking of. Let Me remove it, and bring that change in you, so we can heat you up again with the refining fire and get on to the next issue. I'll keep bringing you back to the same area of your character that needs to change until you get it right. I know you want to change, allow Me to do the changing, one flaw at a time.

December 2

Psalm 43:5

Why art thou cast down, O my soul? and why art thou disquieted within me? Hope in God: for I shall yet praise him, who is the health of my countenance, and my God. KJV

Why are you down in the dumps, dear soul? Fix my eyes on God -- soon I'll be praising again. He puts a smile on my face. He's my God. The Message

Lift your face towards Me. Lift it up. Sing a praise and worship song. Let this world's troubling of your soul melt from your spirit -- as Mine anoints and helps you. I am your God. That means I cover and protect you. Bring your troubles to Me. I want to turn the page. I want to bring you joy as you pass through this world and work amongst this generation for souls for My kingdom. I am your God. You are Mine. That means I treasure every tear you shed. Do you know I keep each one in a bottle? I am your God. I named you before time began. I formed you in the palm of My hands. Do you know that I am aware of every thought that goes through your mind? I really do hear you when you speak to Me. I respond many times with singing over you. That's right. I sing over you. You bring Me joy. Your fellowship with Me brings Me more joy than you can ever imagine. Speak to your soul, command it to look to Me for hope and I will bring health and dignity to you. Watch your countenance change as I draw you closer and closer to your destiny and purpose.

December 3

Luke 12:32

Fear not, little flock; for it is your Father's good pleasure to give you the kingdom. KJV

Don't be afraid of missing out. You're my dearest friends! The Father wants to give you the very kingdom itself. The Message

Jesus was pointing out how fear creeps in when your concerns are more on what you can get, than what you can give. Always look for opportunities to give. Giving opens the door to prosperity and a flow through of blessings. You won't miss out on a thing. You can never ever out give Me. When you give in My name, you open a flood gate into your life. Just remember don't close the hand that is giving out. Keep it open as wide as you do the hand that is receiving the blessing. This is a powerful revelation of kingdom living. Never allow fear to cause you to stop giving. Lack of faith, or distrust in Me, opens the door to the spirit of fear. Run with Me on this. See if I don't open the windows of heaven and pour you out a blessing, that your house could not contain it.

Proverb 4:18

The ways of right-living people glow with light; the longer they live, the brighter they shine.   The Message

There is a reason they glow with light. It is because My Son resides in them. As you live longer for Christ, there is less of the 'flesh' and its residue in the countenance and more of Christ is able to be seen. Never underestimate one day of living for Christ. Each task, each victory, they are all to mold and shape you and make you more like Him. Consider, Moses had to mask his face after being in My physical presence. My presence has an effect on you. The more you enter My presence, spiritually, the more it will display in you and through you, physically. You want to shine in your generation, live right and spend some time with Me.

1 Corinthians 11:3

But I would have you know, that the head of every man is Christ; and the head of the woman is the man; and the head of Christ is God. KJV

Paul is writing to bring some order into the church. The church in Corinth had many confusions. This was one of them. A man who disrespects Christ, disrespects God, this is true. And you know the outcome of that. A woman who disrespects her husband, disrespects God also. She becomes an ugly sight to others as well. She loses her beauty. It's like looking at a woman who has shaven her head and lost her hair. The husband is to cover the wife. The wife is to respect him as the head, so that he can meet the needs of the home. How can a man cover a woman who argues constantly, or complains that he is not good enough? He is good enough, since God gave him to you. When you see a fault, pray for him, he needs it. If you will back him, run in the direction he is running, your road, your tasks in life, will become much more bearable, and more fine-tuned. Homes running in different directions don't work. The man will eventually give up to an overbearing wife. He will never become who I have created him to be. Their destiny as a couple will be lost. Trust Me to guide and direct your husband. Trust your husband and I will mold and shape him into a loving spouse who can cover you and embolden you through many things in your life. Give Me a commitment today, and turn around in six months, and you won't even recognize the beauty that has blossomed in you and your countenance. Tuck away the 'how to' videos you cling to just to find beauty tips from the world. Submit to, serve and love your husband and see what I will do.

December 6

1 Corinthians 10:13

There hath no temptation taken you but such as is common to man: but God is faithful, who will not suffer you to be tempted above that you are able; but will with the temptation also make a way to escape, that ye may be able to bear it.   KJV

Regardless of its source, no temptation can take you. I will always provide you a way out. I am your deed to victory. When confused and not sure how to get out, just stop, take a look around, even pray, your escape is there and will become evident. The devil is a master at confusion. Usually confusion is the only thing that keeps you from seeing your escape route. Many times you'll fall. When you fall, jump back up, through repentance. My grace is not a sleazy grace, a get out of jail free card, nor an excuse to sin. My grace however is sufficient for those that seek My face. I want to teach you to be an overcomer. Your victories are sure in Me. I want to make you strong and able to bear many things. I build you so I can use you as a mighty warrior in My kingdom. I build you to watch you mature as a Christian on the earth, and to become an awesome saint - to walk the streets of gold in heaven, in fellowship with Me, for eternity. Eternity is forever.

December 7

1 Corinthians 10:3-6

And did all eat the same spiritual meat;

And did all drink the same spiritual drink; for they drank of that spiritual Rock that followed them; and that Rock was Christ.

But with many of them God was not well pleased; for they were overthrown in the wilderness.

Now these things were our examples, to the intent we should not lust after evil things, as they also lusted.   KJV

It was because of their lust; their faith was eroded. The warning here is - for your example - so you don't suffer the same fate. Their lust for the 'former' life - the leeks and foods, the idols, the life styles, the things back there, opened the door to the spirit of fear. When faith erodes, fear floods in. So many never see what I want to do in their lives because of fear. Water flowed from that Rock. Their thirst was quenched. As they were guided in the desert I met all of their needs. However, fear took the place of faith. When they took their eyes off of Me and placed them on Egypt, the old life, the former things, they didn't see the water flow from the Rock. They didn't see the Red Sea parted. They didn't even see My fire by night and cloud cover by day. They never recovered and weren't able to enter the promised land. When you find yourself losing your way, unable to see Me in your circumstance, maybe it's because lust is blinding you, and you have allowed fear to enter in and separate you from My blessing. Join Me in morning prayer, let Me help you with this.

December 8

Hebrews 6:18-19,20

That by two immutable things, in which it is impossible for God to lie, we might have a strong consolation, who have fled for refuge to lay hold upon the hope set before us:

Which hope we have as an anchor of the soul, both sure and steadfast, and which entereth into that within the veil;

...even Jesus   KJV

There are two unchangeable (immutable) things that will always birth hope in your life. Number one is My promise, number two is My oath. I am not a man, I cannot lie. This is your 'strong' consolation, I give you My Word. The hope that is birthed has a name. Hope is a person; His name is Jesus. Jesus entered the heavenly temple before you, as a forerunner, as a high priest, as a sacrifice for your sins. The power released spiritually in the resurrection of Jesus from the dead is so much more than you can ever grasp. I have promised you eternal life. I have promised you salvation through Christ. I give you My oath that I will fulfill My promises. In times of trial especially, remember this Hope. Hope will be the anchor of your soul. Anchors cannot be broken, even under tremendous pressure. Hold tight, with both hands, to this Hope.

December 9

2 Corinthians 5:7

For we walk by faith, not by sight. KJV

It's what we trust in but don't see yet that keeps us going.

The Message

living our lives in a manner consistent with our confident belief in God's promises   AMP

Faith is critical to your salvation. Without faith you will not make heaven. I find no pleasure, nor fellowship, with one who will not trust Me. I find it an affront to Me, you call Me a liar, when you do not trust My promises to you. Faithful is one who believes in the 'truthfulness' of Me. I have a plan. You are a person with destiny. You have a purpose, designed by Me, beyond this circumstance in your life today. You have to be willing to possess your tomorrows if you want your destiny. The Israelites in the desert did not have that willingness. They never possessed their promised land. You have to take possession, it won't be handed to you. You have to learn how to fight the enemy. There will always be good times living for Me. Don't let the enemy blind your vision. Fight for what's yours. Do not let your future die because of a lack of faith and trust. Have faith in My ability to provide for you. You can entirely miss what I am doing, if you simply refuse to step out into the unknown by faith.

December 10

Matthew 22:2, 5

The kingdom of heaven is like unto a certain King, which made a marriage for his son.

But they made light of it ... KJV

When invited to a wedding, most consider that pretty important, and that's at an earthly marriage. How much more important the marriage of My Son to His bride, the bride who happens to be the church, that's you! Do not make light of it, as so many do. Do not allow farm, nor merchandise keep you from this. Yes, go into the highway and the byway and compel them to come in. The hope is many will come. The reality is many will not. For many are called, but few are chosen. And also, few choose to come. Will you?

December 11

Matthew 4:12-17

Now when Jesus had heard that John was cast into prison, he departed into Galilee.

And leaving Nazareth, he came and dwelt in Capernaum, which is upon the sea coast, in the borders of Zabulon and Nephthalim:

That it might be fulfilled which was spoken by Esaias the prophet saying,

The land of Zabulon, and the land of Nephthalim, by the way of the sea, beyond Jordan, Galilee of the Gentiles;

The people which sat in darkness saw great light; and to them which sat in the region and shadow of death light is sprung up.

From that time Jesus began to preach, and to say, Repent; for the kingdom of heaven is at hand. KJV

John was arrested. Jesus picked up where John the Baptist left off. I will always make a way for the sinner to repent. John the Baptist was a faithful warrior. The world, especially the religious world, hated John. They will hate you because of Me. I even sent My Son because they killed the prophets, my ambassadors. Then they killed My Son, trying to silence Me dealing with their hearts on the sin in their lives. Many will over-react with you, when you speak My Word to them. However, they still need to hear it. Go ye. Tell them for Me. This is where the light comes on for so many in the midst of their darkness. A bright light that will spring up and deliver them from the shadow of death. Jesus is that light. The kingdom of heaven is at hand. Will you be My hands and feet and go into all the world preaching and teaching in My name?

Matthew 21:38, 45

But when the husbandmen saw the son, they said among themselves, This is the heir; come, let us kill him, and let us seize on his inheritance,

And when the chief priests and Pharisees had heard his parables, they perceived that he spake of them.   KJV

December 12

Matthew 5:3

Blessed are the poor in spirit; for theirs is the kingdom of heaven. KJV

Thinking you're poor in spirit? Feeling low, down and out? A perfect place for you to have more of Me. The interpretation of The Message bible says - "You're blessed when you're at the end of your rope. With less of you there is more of God and his rule." You can probably understand that interpretation the best. There are many factors in your world today to pull you down, besides the spiritual warfare you endure. When you feel this way, take time to meet with Me. Find a place to be by yourself with Me and vocalize your feelings out loud. Watch what I will do. The page will turn in your spirit quite quickly. Many times, I am able to turn the page in the issues as well. Always remember I take time quite frequently to change circumstances, but I will never allow more than you can bear. Many times, it is because there is more going on that is affected by the changes than you understand. Let Me do this from My perspective, I can see the entire picture, when you cannot at this time. Trust Me with this.

Psalm 104:34

My meditation of him shall be sweet; I will be glad in the Lord.
KJV

Take time to meditate on Me. Take time to rejoice in Me. Let Me
show you what relationship with Me can do for sweetening up your
life and ushering in a gladness of heart for your countenance. Life is
precious. Life is sweet. You do belong to Me. Dwell on these things.
I have a joy unspeakable for those that will run the race with Me and
finish their course designed by Me, your God.

December 14

Hebrews 1:9

Thou hast loved righteousness, and hated iniquity; therefore God,
even thy God, hath anointed thee with the oil of gladness above thy
fellows.   KJV

My Son. I spoke these words to My Son. Paul recorded them for Me
that you could know. My Son, Jesus is the only name under heaven
whereby you can be saved. You must repent and surrender your life
to Christ. There is no other way unto salvation. Sin separates. Christ
is the sacrifice, the blood sacrifice, required for the cleansing of sin.
When you repent and surrender yourself, think of the soldier on the
battlefield. As he raises his arms, he lets down his possessions,
including all of his resources and is at the behest of a new army. He
does what his new king commands. He is submitted. Unlike this
soldier on the battlefield, you are walking into blessing on the other
side. Never look back! Lift your arms, surrender, and trust Christ.
As you embrace a love for Christ - He will impart in you a love for
right - a disdain for evil - and anoint you with the oil of gladness,
which is My Holy Spirit. This is regeneration.

Acts 9:6

Lord, what wilt thou have me to do?   KJV

I had to knock Saul down and blind him to rescue the next Christian he had his heart set on putting to death. Saul was a hard man. A religious zealot. Beware of doing the things you do, in My name. Make sure it is Me who gave you the task to do. Saul was in a habit of being so in charge and powerful, he was indignant that these Christians would not obey him and his peers, and stop the teaching of something he knew nothing about. Instead of finding out what was right, he insisted he was right. Instead of taking the time to inquire, he saw his 'position' in question as many Jews were becoming Christians. Political correctness, political pressure- it's so loud - so loud that you won't take the time to listen to the issue at hand. Instead of standing for what is right, you can find yourself favoring a 'friend's' position in an argument or circumstance, just to keep your own position in life. Don't do that. Stay prayed up, listen to Me, not to your friends or your paycheck. Listen to Me. When you do have to make a stand against something, many times I can bless you right where you stand, many times it will cost you much. But never despair. You live by My economy, not the world's. I'll carry you when no one else takes a second glance, only because you stood for what was right. This is your reasonable service. Don't put Me in the position where I have to knock you down and blind you - just to get your attention- so you can do right. Ask Me ahead of time, "Lord, what will you have me do today?"

Deuteronomy 33:26-27

The eternal God is thy refuge, and underneath are the everlasting arms: and he shall thrust out the enemy from before thee; and shall say, Destroy them. KJV

There is none like God, Jeshurun, riding to your rescue through the skies, his dignity haloed by clouds. The ancient God is home on a foundation of everlasting arms. He drove out the enemy before you and commanded, "Destroy!" The Message

There is a spiritual warfare for your soul. You cannot see it with human eyes, but you can see the affects. Of course, you feel the effects as well. 99.9% of your battles in life will be in your mind. The enemy fights dirty. They are wickedness and they are in high places. They are real entities, not just comic book material. They work against you for one purpose and one purpose only. They want to destroy you. I do not tell you this to strike fear in you. I tell you this so that you will be vigilant. Your enemy is real. Be sober. Watch and be discrete. Use words that build others and this will build you as well. Your words are so powerful. I want to impress that on you today. Your words are so powerful. Stop speaking in the negative. Instead of getting angry and saying "no way" when someone asks you for something. If you want to think about it, start by saying, "we'll see." Give yourself time to process things before you speak negatively. Find a pad answer that will keep you from being negative constantly. It is hard to take back words that are spoken. Many times, the very thing you said "no way" to - is so very simple for you to lend a hand in. Many times, I have sent that person to you for the request to be fulfilled. Don't let the enemy rip you off of a blessing by blessing others. Don't let the enemy get you into such bad habits that you no longer respond in the affirmative because of all of the "let downs" in life. Many times, the "let downs" were not really what they seemed to be. Slow down and process things before you respond. The enemy is real. He tries to make you react quickly which affects many things in life. This is a major strategy against your soul. Remember- slow to speak. It will help you take time so that you can learn to speak in the positive more often. I can move in this area in your life, bring it to the altar. I'll help you guard your lips.

December 17

Deuteronomy 33:29

A people saved by God! The Shield who defends you, the Sword who brings triumph. KJV

Victory truly is Mine. Even in your life, I take ownership of it. Why do I do that? Because you are Mine. You have been set aside for purpose and destiny. Do not believe that anything happens in your life without My covering and allowing it. Many times, you reap what you sow, many times it is an enemy attack, many times it is just living life in a fallen world and you and yours being affected by it. But I have your destiny and purpose, your end, all in the palm of My hand. I have a plan, Saint. I have a plan. Eyes forward, think of heaven. Let Me fight the battle, you just remember to place it in My hands, daily. Put it there through prayer, and attitude, and faith. Faith moves mountains, and it allows Me to move in your life. Without faith, My hands are tied. I cannot violate you. Surrender this to Me. Bring it to the altar, don't keep picking it back up and trying to fix it your way. Allow Me to move. I have a plan.

Psalms 84:10

For a day in thy courts is better than a thousand. I had rather be a door-keeper in the house of my God, than to dwell in the tents of wickedness. KJV

Take time with Me, precious saint. Your head can be turned so easily. Stay in My Word, read it daily. I have much to teach you. Pray every day. Speak with Me throughout your day. Draw close. I have created and designed you for fellowship with Me. Nothing else will work, nothing else will satisfy. As you draw close -- the joy of My kingdom will fill you more and more. Your spiritual growth will astound you. Regrets are awash on the beaches of those who have walked away. You came out of that life because of the afflictions. Don't look back. Press in. Look forward. Grow in Me.

Proverbs 11:22

As a jewel of gold in a swine's snout, so is a fair woman which is without discretion. KJV

Discretion is a virtue needed to accent a woman's beauty. Without it, her beauty is mocked. Her old age will come early and her wickedness will wreak from her lips. Discretion is a definitive quality of behavior and speech. Be a discrete woman, she uses a guardedness in the words she uses, just so to avoid causing an offense or revealing information that should be kept private. Be discrete even with your husband. Why offend him, when you can build him? Stop and listen to the way you talk. Pay attention to the way you deliver remarks. Hear what you say. Ask Me. I will help you with this. Change the foaming at your mouth of callousness and carelessness to a beautiful song and sweet aroma to those I place in your path. Be kind today.

December 20

Ephesians 2:10

For we are his workmanship   KJV

You have been created by Me. You have been designed and called for a specific purpose. Your purpose is on planet earth for right now. I have placed in you a desire to serve. Hell fights you on that. Many times, the menial things and duties of life make you think you are of no use or purpose. I tell you it is the ones involved in the labor that I will come back for. The high fliers fizzle out. Look around, they burn for a season, and then they are gone. Take time and ask Me in the morning to help you with your 'to do list'. I'll be glad to be involved in your day and help you rest in the evening knowing that you did your best in serving Me. I am not a mute idol that does not speak to His people. I am not a deaf statue that does not hear when you call. I hear and I speak and I use My hand to bring you strength. Change your habits to include Me, run in My will and your days will be altered forever.

December 21

Psalms 42:5

Why art thou cast down, O my soul? and why art thou disquieted in me? hope thou in God; for I shall yet praise him for the help of his countenance.   KJV

He puts a smile on my face. He's my God.   The Message

I have the remedy. You don't have to come up with the plan. You must praise Me before the battle. There's something very therapeutic for you in praise. Get loud and get definitive. Get aggressive with praise. Get your praise on. For breakthrough stand clear of emotions. David commanded his soul. Sometimes you have to tell yourself. Command your soul to act right. Praise should be emotional - but it's not just emotion. You must not allow emotions to run your life. You overcome with praise. Worship for who I am, praise for what I have done. I am -- the mightiest, mightier than your situation. This will take the focus off of you. No one can make you get dressed. You decide to get dressed. You decide to put your armor on every day. You decide to put your praise on every day. This will release My power in your life.

December 22

2 Peter 1:3

According as his divine power hath given unto us all things that pertain unto life and godliness KJV

2 Peter 1:3-4

Everything that goes into a life of pleasing God has been miraculously given to us by getting to know, personally and intimately, the One who invited us to God. The best invitation we ever received! We were also given absolutely terrific promises to pass on to you -- your tickets to participation in the life of God after you turned your back on a world corrupted by lust.

The Message

I do not need to give you more, I have given you everything you need. I want to give you something deeper. Love is deep. Lust is not.

Love overcomes and penetrates, seeks and builds, works hard and long to break through and change the human heart. Sounding brass and smoke and mirrors and counterfeits - they do not. When I spoke so often on idols in the scriptures; it was because I knew they stood in the way of My people and Me. They still do. Your idol in your world may not be a totem pole or a buddha statuette made by human hands. However, your idol is anything that separates you from Me - that you turn to for your needs. Not every distraction is an idol. But every idol is a distraction from Me. If you would love Me and seek Me, the rest would fall by the wayside. Press in through prayer. Wake up early in the morning so you have time for Me. I will bring you strength. Seek Me with all your heart. I want to mold and shape you for a destiny far beyond what you have ever imagined.

December 23

Colossians 3:13

And above all these things put on charity, which is the bond of perfectness.   KJV

Remember when Paul speaks the word "charity" - he is referring to "love". Put love on. Dress in it. Take time to remember it's there. Love people. They need that. Love people. You need that. You cannot feed My sheep without love. They will choke and die every single time. Without love you are nothing. You are naked when you forget to put it on in the mornings. Cover yourself with it. You look gorgeous in it. They look great through your eyes when your eyes are dressed in it as well. Forgive and let go. Pick up love. It will change your life. It will change your world. It will change your destiny. Love changes people - period. Well -- it changed you!

December 24

Proverbs 15:15

..he that is of a merry heart hath a continual feast.   KJV

Your countenance changes things. Your faith in Me changes your countenance. People who are angry with Me, generally carry a heavy countenance. People who are frustrated with how I do things generally pout and throw fits, which leads to ugliness and poverty. When you trust Me in all of your circumstances - even your gait in the morning and throughout the day will change. This will wrought blessing. Think like this. If you were the owner of a business, would you hire or promote a guy who is always throwing a fit? or the guy who has a handle on things and a good attitude no matter what comes his way? Usually the latter of the two. Someone who can handle difficult circumstances is more apt to make right decisions and cause the business to prosper. This in turn blesses his home, his life, while the first man is soon without an income or home or family. In other words, he is his own demise. Look at Me. Trust Me. It will change your countenance. Smile at Me. This is life. Trials and turns, unexpected circumstances, issues beyond your control, serving people you don't feel like serving, all of this, but through Me and with Me, a life well lived and filled with blessing. Take time, repent of bad attitudes, turn towards Me, watch your day change, watch your life change.

December 25

John 15:18

If the world hate you, ye know, that the world hated me before it hated you. KJV

Paul didn't care what the world threw at him. Because he had conversion. He got locked up, he saw jailers get saved. He was dragged before the powerful, he testified openly. He was beaten and left for dead, he escaped and nourished the churches. He was ran out of town, he built another church. He was shipwrecked, he preached Jesus to the natives. He took Me where ever he went. Do you? You won't be able to take what the world will throw at you until you are sold out to Christ. If you are not doing it for Me, you will fail. Pure and simple.

December 26

Colossians 4:5

Walk in wisdom toward them that are without, redeeming the time. KJV

Use your heads as you live and work among outsiders. Don't miss a trick. Make the most of every opportunity. The Message

Redeem the time, don't miss opportunities, take time to witness and declare My Word. It is a lost and dying generation. It is a generation that does not begin their school morning with prayer. Many have parents that do not take them in prayer before they go to bed at night. Many do not even know they can bring their troubles to Me and find rest. You are My voice. You are My witness. Take time to share and let them know that I am the Lord. Tell them I am God and willing to change their lives. Be that seed in this generation. They long to know Me. To many I am the unknown God. Share the gospel of Jesus Christ whenever you can. He died and rose again to bring life and life more abundantly. It's true.

Colossians 4:6

Let your speech be alway with grace, seasoned with salt, that ye may know how ye ought to answer every man.   KJV

I know it is hard to decide how to answer every man. You have not the discernment all of the time. Error on the side of grace when you are unsure. Be slow to answer. Be angry, but don't sin. Anger is a natural emotion, I gave you that. But it is not something to be used as an excuse for zero self-control. Do not let your emotions rule your speech. You lose every single time. Pray about this. I will bring growth and maturity in this area of your life; however, you must contend for it. It is very hard to take back words that are spoken. They cut deep many times, hurting those you really love. Take a step back, wait for a bit, and speak when you know it is right. Salt does cleanse, and hurts, and sometimes it is needed in the conversation. Always remember, you do not have to speak everything that pops into your mind. Be wise, speak little. Be kind, show grace.

December 28

Romans 11:29

God's gifts and God's call are under full warranty -- never canceled, never rescinded.   The Message

Romans 12:2 be ye transformed by the renewing of your mind. KJV

The light of Christ is such a light that it outshines the dark. Gone are the days of the depression that would engulf and cripple you. Here are the days of life and life more abundantly. For without Christ there was no light in your life. The light was dimmed and hard to see. Perhaps think of it as a door shut upon it so that it could barely flicker through the cracks. Ah! The light of Christ. Bask in it. For when that light burst open upon your life, when you finally yielded your life to Me, that light flooded and renewed you. The tears you wept were tears of joy. Remember. Joy, such as you had never felt. Joy, such that only increases as the days with Me accumulate. I will never leave you, nor forsake you. You can freely trust in the love of Christ. You can freely trust in Me to care for you, yes, even when you screw up. God helps those who help themselves? That statement is a bit loose on truth. God helps those who ask Him for His help. Now that is what you have found to be true. Remember. And so ask daily. Lord? I need you. Lord... I need you. Lord, I need you. And you really really do. And I really really help. With each ache and pain in your body, give it to Me. With each trial and temptation, you must give it to Me, or you truly will, without a doubt, fail. You always used to tell Me, "Lord, you know I don't do well on tests, I usually fail." You really used to pray like that. Now, you have entered into a bit of maturity, for My glory's sake. Now you often pray, "Lord, please help me, I know I can do this with You involved." And boom, that's where I have been able to move. You enable Me. So, I would say, continue to grow up my dear. Learn to trust Me. Speak faith. I want that. And that is when I can move. Remember. Thank Me for helping. You have so much to learn.

December 29

Glorious

Psalms 145:5

Your beauty and splendor have everyone talking; I compose songs on your wonders.   The Message

I will speak of the glorious honor of thy majesty, and thy wondrous works.   KJV

Two thousand years after the birth of My Son. They are still talking. When earth met heaven, the skies opened and My glory was revealed and the shepherds went as quickly as possible to witness this miracle. They left talking and witnessing. I so expect, in that same manner, after you have received the visitation of My glory and the personal relationship with My Son, for you to go, and witness. Share my Word. Let them know. Speak it out. For how would they know unless they are told. Be My hands and feet, and I will bring the anointing you desire and have requested in prayer day after day. It is in the spoken word.

December 30

Unsearchable

Psalms 145:3

..and his greatness is unsearchable.   KJV

There are no boundaries to His greatness.   The Message

Unsearchable. What a huge word for you. Your mind cannot comprehend. Your eyes have not seen. Your ears have never heard. My greatness is so vast, the human brain cannot fathom.

You are so important to Me. I have molded and shaped you. I have called you by name. Do you hear Me when I call? I hold your life in the palm of My hands. Follow Me. Place Me first in your life, that My will for you is fulfilled. I will make you new. Trust. Trust like a child, trust always that I will never leave you nor forsake you. I am that presence on your right side, gently pressing you on, guiding you to do right and not evil all the days of your life, that you would dwell in My house forever.

Psalms 145:20 God sticks by all those who love Him. The Message

Psalms 139:6

I look behind me and you're there, then up ahead and you're there, too -- your reassuring presence, coming and going. This is too much, too wonderful -- I can't take it all in.

The Message

Discipline brings obedience. As your obedience becomes habit it becomes natural. Because of the company you keep, and the places you have been taught to frequent, the roads you choose, you become happier to bring Me along. I'm always here, however, your acknowledgement of My presence is not always there. Walk with Me into a new season. Follow Me. Talk to Me, out loud. Do not keep Me and our relationship secret from your friends and family. Meet with Me in the mornings. Let's do this together. Watch how your life will change.

If you have read this far, and do not know Jesus Christ as your personal Lord and Savior? May I invite you to pray a simple prayer and ask Him into your heart? Of course, read it first, see if you agree, and then say it 'out loud' to your heavenly Father.

Dear God, I pray that you would forgive me a sinner. I am so sorry and I repent of my sin and ask you to come into my heart. I know Jesus, shed his blood and died on the cross, and then He rose from the dead – 3 days later, so that I could have resurrection power over my sin, conquer death, as He did, and be saved. I want that eternal life with you, that you promise. Would you be Lord of my life and help me to learn what that means? I surrender to you my broken life today, in Jesus's mighty name, thank you.

CPSIA information can be obtained
at www.ICGtesting.com
Printed in the USA
LVHW010008260420
654436LV00002B/271

—— (1992), 'Os Mebengokre Kayapó: história e mudança social, de comunidades autônomas para a coexistência interétnica', in M. Carneiro da Cunha (ed.), *História dos índios no Brasil* (São Paulo: Companhia das Letras/Fapesp/SMC), 311–38.

—— (1995), 'Social Body and Embodied Subject: Bodiliness, Subjectivity, and Sociality among the Kayapo', *Cultural Anthropology*, 10(2): 143–70.

TURNER, V. (1974), *Dramas, Fields, and Metaphors* (Cornell: Cornell University Press).

—— (1979), 'Dramatic Ritual/Ritual Drama: Performative and Reflexive Anthropology', *Kenyon Review* (NS), 1(3): 80–93.

URBAN, G. (1986), 'Ceremonial Dialogues in Native South America', *American Anthropologist*, 88: 371–86.

—— (1988*a*), 'Ritual Wailing in Amerindian Brazil', *American Ethnologist*, 90: 385–400.

—— (1988*b*), 'The Linguistic Anthropology of Native South America', *Annual Reviews of Anthropology*, 17: 283–307.

—— (1991), *A Discourse-Centered Approach to Culture: Native South American Myths and Rituals* (Austin: University of Texas Press).

VAN DE PORT, M. (1998), *Gypsies, Wars and Other Instances of the Wild: Civilisation and its Discontents in a Serbian Town* (Amsterdam: Amsterdam University Press).

VAN DER HAMMEN, M. C. (1992), *El manejo del mundo: naturaleza y sociedad entre los Yukuna de la Amazonia colombiana* (Estudios en la Amazonia Colombiana 4; Santafé de Bogotá: Tropenbos Colombia).

VELLARD, J. (1965), *Histoire du curare: Les poisons de chasse en Amérique du Sud* (Paris: Gallimard).

VILAÇA, A. (1992), *Comendo como gente: formas do canibalismo wari'.* (Rio de Janeiro: Editora da UFRJ).

—— (1995), 'O sistema do parentesco wari', in E. Viveiros de Castro (ed.), *Antropologia do Parentesco: Estudos Amerindios* (Rio de Janeiro: Editora da UFRJ), 265–319.

VIVEIROS DE CASTRO, E. (1979), 'A fabricação do corpo na sociedade xinguana', *Boletim do Museu Nacional* (NS), 32: 40–9.

—— (1987), 'Sociedades Minimalistas: A Propósito de um Livro de Peter Rivière', *Anuário Antropológico*, 85: 265–82.

—— (1992), *From the Enemy's Point of View: Humanity and Divinity in an Amazonian Society* (Chicago: University of Chicago Press).

—— (1993), 'Alguns aspectos da afinidade no dravidianato Amazónico', in E. Viveiros de Castro and M. Carneiro da Cunha (eds.), Amazônia: etnologia e história (São Paulo: NHII/Universidade de São Paulo and FAPESP), 149–210

—— (1995*a*), 'Pensando o parentesco ameríndio', in Viveiros de Castro (1995*b*), 7–24.

—— (ed.) (1995*b*), *Antropologia do parentesco: estudos ameríndios* (Rio de Janeiro: Editora UFRJ.)

—— (1996*a*), 'Os pronomes cosmológicos e o perspectivismo Ameríndio', *Mana*, 2(2): 115–44.

—— (1996*b*), 'Images of Nature and Society in Amazonian Ethnology', *Annual Review of Anthropology*, 25: 179–200.

—— (1998*a*), 'Cosmological Deixis and Amerindian Perspectivism', *Journal of the Royal Anthropological Institute*, 4(3): 469–88.

—— (1998*b*), 'Dravidian and Related Kinship Systems', in T. Trautmann, M. Godelier, and F. Tjon Sie Fat (eds.), *Transformations of Kinship* (Washington, DC: Smithsonian Institution), 332–85.

VIVEIROS DE CASTRO, E. and FAUSTO, C. (1993), 'La Puissance et l'acte: la parenté dans les basses terres d'Amérique du Sud' (Special Edition of *L'Homme*, 126–8, vol. XXXIII; Paris: École des Hautes Études en Sciences Sociales), 141–70.

WAGLEY, C. (1977), *Welcome of Tears: The Tapirapé of Central Brazil* (New York: Oxford University Press).

WAGNER, R. (1978), *Lethal Speech: Daribi Myth as Symbolic Obviation* (Ithaca: Cornell University Press).

—— (1981 [1975]), *The Invention of Culture* (Chicago: University of Chicago Press).

—— (1991), 'The Fractal Person', in M. Godelier and M. Strathern (eds.), *Big Men and Great Men: Personification of Power in Melanesia* (Cambridge: Cambridge University Press), 159–73.

WALTZ, C. (1980), 'Notes on Guanano Kinship', manuscript (Summer Institute of Linguistics, Bogotá).

WALTZ, NATHAN, and WALTZ, CAROLYN (n.d.), 'The Uanano', manuscript (Summer Institute of Linguistics, Bogotá).

WEBER, M. (1992 [1930]), *The Protestant Ethic and the Spirit of Capitalism* (London: Routledge).

WHIFFEN, T. (1915), *The Northwest Amazon: Notes of Some Months Spent among Cannibal Tribes* (London: Constable).

WHITAKER, M. P. (1996), 'Ethnography as Learning: A Wittgensteinian Approach to Writing Ethnographic Accounts', *Anthropological Quarterly*, 69(1): 1–13.

WHITEHEAD, N. L. (1990), 'The Snake Warriors—Sons of the Tiger's Teeth: A Descriptive Analysis of Carib Warfare: 1500–1820', in J. Haas (ed.), *The Anthropology of War* (Cambridge: Cambridge University Press), 146–70.

—— (1996), *An Oral History of the Patamuna, Yawong Valley, Guyana* (Georgetown: Walter Roth Museum).

—— (1997), 'Monstrosity and Marvel: Symbolic Convergence and Mimetic Elaboration in Trans-Cultural Representation', *Studies in Travel Writing*, 1: 72–96.

—— (1998), *The Discoverie of the Large, Rich and Bewtiful Empire of Guiana by Sir Walter Ralegh*, edited, annotated and transcribed (Exploring Travel Series, vol. 1; Manchester: Manchester University Press; and American Exploration & Travel Series, vol. 71; Norman: Oklahoma University Press).

—— (forthcoming), *Kanaimà: A Poetic of Violent Death* (Durham, NC: Duke University Press).

WHITTEN, N. (1976), *Sacha Runa* (Urbana: University of Illinois Press).

WITTGENSTEIN, L. (1953), *Philosophical Investigations*, transl. G. E. M. Anscombe (Oxford: Blackwell).

—— (1958a), *Philosophical Investigations* (New York: Macmillan).

—— (1958b), *The Blue and Brown Books: Preliminary Studies for the 'Philosophical Investigations'* (New York: Harper Colophon Books).

WUSTMANN, E. (1960), *Yahuá: Die Blasrohr-Indianer* (Radebeul: Neumann Verlag).

YALMAN, N. (1962), 'The Structure of the Sinhalese Kindred: A Re-examination of the Dravidian Terminology', *American Anthropologist*, 64: 548–75.

—— (1971), *Under the Bo Tree: Studies in Caste, Kinship and Marriage in the Interior of Ceylon* (Berkeley: University of California Press).

YAMAJI, K. (1994), 'Plant and Gender: The Reproductive Image of Mother in the Nakanai of Papua New Guinea', in *Gender and Fertility in Melanesia* (Nishinomiya: Kwansei Gakuin University Press), 13–46.

YDE, J. (1948), 'The Regional Distribution of South American Blowgun Types', *Journal de la Société des Américanistes*, 37: 275–317.

YOST, J. and KELLEY, P. (1983), 'Shotguns, Blowguns and Spears: The Analysis of Technological Efficiency', in R. Hames and W. Vickers (eds.), *Adaptive Responses of Native Amazonians* (New York: Academic Press), 189–224.

ZERRIES, O. (1984), 'Die Rolle des Ameisenbüren in Vorstellung und Ritual ausserandinischer Indianer: Eineethnozoologische Studie', *Zeitschrift für Ethnologie*, 109(2): 181–229.

ZIMAN, J. (1978), *Reliable Knowledge: An Exploration of the Grounds for Belief in Science* (Cambridge: Cambridge University Press).

INDEX